The Nether Shore of No More Partings

THE STORY OF WILLIAM THORNWALL DAVIS

ROBERT G. DAVIS

THE NETHER SHORE OF NO MORE PARTINGS:
THE STORY OF WILLIAM THORNWALL DAVIS

COPYEDITING/DESIGN/PRODUCTION: WILLIAM VAN DOREN AND LAURA SUTHERLAND

COMMISSIONED PHOTOGRAPHY: MONICA PEDYNKOWSKI

PHOTOS, PAGES 26–27: *MILITARY SURGEON*, VOL. 19, NO. 1 (JULY 1906)

ALL OTHER IMAGES COURTESY OF THE DAVIS FAMILY

Publisher's Cataloging-In-Publication Data
(Prepared by The Donohue Group, Inc.)

Names: Davis, Robert G., 1945-
Title: The nether shore of no more partings : the story of William
    Thornwall Davis / Robert G. Davis.
Other Titles: Story of William Thornwall Davis
Description: Charlottesville, VA : Robert G. Davis, [2017]
Identifiers: ISBN 978-0-692-90554-8
Subjects: LCSH: Davis, William Thornwall, 1877-1944. | United States.
    Army--Medical personnel--Biography. | Ophthalmologists--Washington
    (D.C.)--Biography. | United States--History, Military--20th century. |
    Davis family. | LCGFT: Biographies.
Classification: LCC UH347.D38 D385 2017 | DDC 355.3/45092--dc23

There are countless individuals in the history of our great country, the United States of America, of such outstanding character, accomplishment, sacrifice and principle that they inspire those same virtues in those whom they touch. Every family lineage has such people. These special people build and bind their families. They help form family foundations for successful and happy lives. They inspire and embolden their progeny to build their families strong and to carry on family traditions of steady character and love. They give us courage, determination and the will to succeed in life.

This is the story of such a man in the family of Davis.

WILLIAM THORNWALL DAVIS
January 24, 1877 – June 16, 1944

HUSBAND OF RENÉE TOLSON DAVIS
FATHER OF WILLIAM J. G. DAVIS, ROGER HASBROUCK DAVIS,
RENÉ SHELDON DAVIS, AND AKIN THORNWALL DAVIS
GRANDFATHER TO EIGHT GRANDCHILDREN

Sources: Recollections and notes from Roger HB. Davis and Akin Thornwall Davis; family stories; National Archives; newspapers; personal genealogical research; and letters between William Thornwall Davis and his son Roger HB. Davis.

Compiled and written by Robert G. Davis, second grandchild of William Thornwall Davis, and son of Roger HB. Davis. Edited by Robert G. Davis and his brother, Roger HB. Davis, Jr., first grandchild of William T. Davis.

Author's note: In this book I refer to William Thornwall Davis variously as William, Lieut. Davis, Captain Davis, Dr. Davis, W.T.D., and Grandpa. I will refer to his wife as Renée and as Grandma. When I say "my Dad" I am referring to my father, Roger HB. Davis.

William Thornton Davis, Jr., was born January 24, 1877, in Little Rock, Arkansas. His mother died shortly thereafter, at age 22, of puerperal fever. His father, William Thornton Davis, was "deeply grieved and fell apart" after her death; he abandoned William, re-married, and died in 1899 at age 52 (born 1846) of heart disease. William Jr. was then 22 years old. His father's widow came to him for financial assistance, even though neither she nor William's father had made any effort to see him or contribute to his welfare while his father was alive. He refused — he wanted nothing to do with his father. Early in his life he changed his middle name from Thornton to Thornwall and dropped the 'Jr.', thus legally changing his name to William Thornwall Davis.

My dad, Roger, Sr., "couldn't recall much about his (his father's) early boyhood to a young man." Therefore, from the sources previously mentioned, we have compiled the following about William's early life.

William's mother, Theresa Akin, was the daughter of David Akin and Sarah Sutton Graham, who was one of six children of Christopher Columbus Graham and Theresa Sutton. William was raised by Sarah (his grandmother), from whom, he said, "I learned my manners and what was expected of a gentleman ... her counsel was so good, so wise and so lasting." They lived in Versailles, Kentucky.

Early years on the family farm:

As a young boy he "borrowed" the young racing mare, rode several miles, bareback, to the county fair, entered the horse race and won. Upon his "triumphant" return home, he was reprimanded and learned that he could have damaged the young mare for the rest of her life. He later said it was a good lesson. He worked hard in the fields, sometimes even sleeping there. He got strong and "wiry."

Early one morning when he was a youngster, he was awakened by some noise outside his home. Looking out his upstairs bedroom window he saw several men, some of whom he recognized, putting on cloaks marked with red crosses, mounting their horses, and riding off ("hooded riders on horseback riding away into darkness"). The next day several black men were found dead, hanging at the local crossroads. He recalled there had been several barn burnings a few days before.

1885

William was eight years old when his great grandfather, Christopher Columbus Graham, then age 100 and still mentally alert and physically active, traveled from Louisville, Kentucky, to Versailles, approximately 60 miles (a long ways in those days), to visit his two daughters, Sarah, with whom William was living, and Teresa Graham Blackburn, who was living in Versailles with her husband, Joseph Blackburn. While there, Dr. Graham spent time with his great-grandson. Later in life William said that of the stories told him by his great grandfather the ones that "made the deepest impression on my boyhood mind were those about the Lincolns, the boy Abe and his parents, Tom and Nancy Lincoln."* During his stay, Dr. Graham "contracted a severe cold, and was just able to make it back to Louisville before taking to bed with a fatal case of bronchitis added to the exhaustion of the years." Christopher Columbus Graham died at the age of 100 years, four months.

1890

After his grandmother's death, when William was 12 or 13, he moved in with some "family friends" and continued working in the farm fields during the summers.

---

*Dr. William Thornwall Davis continued his discussion of what Dr. Graham had told him about the Lincolns. "He told how delighted little Abe was to receive his first book, when [great] Grandfather fished it out of his saddlebags where he had it for him. He often stopped at the Lincoln cabin ... on his journeys. I remember he described the Lincoln house as being a small log cabin pen with a loft and an earthen floor. He was very fond of the boy Lincoln and ... equipped with his hammer and specimen sack, he took Abe with him over the Lincoln farm, searching for interesting geological and ethnological specimens, and in this way the young Lincoln mind was turned away from lowly home influence into the realms of history, natural and political." Dr. Davis declared that he had "often thought since that Grandfather's teachings and character had much to do with the mold and trend of Abraham Lincoln's mind and and after-life." SOURCE: Richard Conn, "Christopher Columbus Graham"

1895
Graduated from Versailles High School (17 or 18 years old).

Dad said that William attended Fishburne Military Academy, although we have not found a record of Fishburne Military Academy in Kentucky. Another account has him going to the Kentucky Military Institute, but this is 58 miles from Versailles. Either way we know he attended a military academy.
    As related by Dad:

> Sometime later, William, in his bedroom at night (he lived on the second floor), heard his family friends downstairs say, "What in the world are we going to do with Billy?" They evidently no longer wished to provide for him. It was his understanding that he had a distant relative, an uncle, U.S. Senator Joseph Blackburn,* Democrat, Kentucky, in Washington, D.C., so he decided to "run away" to find the senator. William was approximately 18. He took a few belongings and set out for Washington on his bicycle. It was winter and very cold. The night he left Versailles was wet and nasty — he made it to a restaurant or bar somewhere and was taken in by a sympathetic prostitute, who took him to her home, fed him, and gave him a night or two of rest before sending him off to Washington. (In his later years he still had respect for prostitutes because "they were honest people.")

> In those days bikes did not have coaster brakes, they were direct drive. While biking down one of the steep hills in the Allegheny Mountains (only dirt roads back then), he lost control, the pedals got away from him, he tried to stay on the road, but eventually he hit one of the drainage trenches and came down in "all kinds of pieces . . . there wasn't a bone on him that wasn't aching." Bruised and scratched, he limped to a nearby town, repaired his bike, and traveled on to Washington.

1896
Soon after arriving in Washington, he made contact in some manner with

---

*Joseph Clay Stiles Blackburn, 1838–1918. Senate years of service: 1885–1897; 1901–1907. Senator Blackburn was W.T.D.'s uncle, although not by blood. Blackburn was married to Teresa Graham, the youngest of Christopher Columbus Graham's six children and sister to W.T.D.'s maternal grandmother, Sarah Sutton Graham.

Senator Blackburn. He met with a Henrietta Blackburn (we do not know her relation to Blackburn — more than likely one of the three children born to Senator Blackburn and his wife, Teresa Graham). "She gave me a big kiss good night and I turned all shades of red." Senator Blackburn made arrangements for William to be a page in the Senate. But William was very hurt because Senator Blackburn did not contact him "for a long time" — Blackburn just let him make his way on his own. "It was a long time before I saw him." Nevertheless he stayed as close as he could to this family all his life. Teresa Graham died in 1899 — we have no information on William's contact with her.

During his time in Washington as a Senate page, he supported himself and continued his education, studying at night as he worked the Senate switchboard as a second job. He recalled an incident when a Senator met with a constituent who had brought an oriental rug as a gift. Before the constituent had a chance to explain why he was visiting, the Senator escorted him along with the rug out the front door of the Capitol. Anyone bringing a gift is asking for something. Grandpa told my father this story in 1936 and added, "You won't find a Congressman doing that today."

He lived in a rooming house in north Washington at the end of an electric streetcar line (the end of Georgia Avenue, out in the country — he couldn't afford anything closer). When he had a function to attend, he would take the long trolley ride to his rooming house, shave, clean up, and immediately ride back into the city. He told of arriving at his room in the early morning after an all-night dance party, changing clothes and taking off for work. He spoke of being lonely, since he seldom joined the "boys" in late night partying. He said, "They were doing things I thought were not proper. I felt that maybe I was wrong but concluded years later I was right."

1897

Entered Columbian University medical school (later George Washington University, in downtown D.C.) night school. In those days students went directly from high school into medical school. He later remarked, "If it weren't for the bars where you could go to buy 5 cent beers and have free food which they would lay out on a table, I never would have made it." As long as you were buying beer you could eat. Once when he had his Thanksgiving dinner at one of the bars where he spent his 5 cents for a beer, he got his slab of turkey (he had to pay extra). Of the cut of turkey served on his plate he said, "I've never seen such a thin slab of turkey in my life, they must have cut it with a straight razor."

William and some other medical students, with approval from the school, took one of the cadavers to his rooming house for home study. It was hung on a wall and one night during a thunderstorm, lights out, the cadaver fell on top of William, arms dangling around his neck — "scared him to hell."

There was a "haunted" old pool hall nearby. People claimed they could hear pool balls clicking at night. On a dare and bet William spent the night in this "haunted" house, only to learn that the clicking was caused by the wicker furniture contracting and expanding.

W.T.D. did not give up his day jobs as he worked his way through school. He was a completely "self-made man." Through all of his many extraordinary efforts, he was undoubtedly inspired by the example of his maternal great grandfather, Christopher Columbus Graham, one of the most distinguished figures in the early history of Kentucky and perhaps the only genuine Renaissance man in Kentucky history. It's probably significant that Graham had been both a physician and a soldier. He was a paleontologist who corresponded with Charles Darwin and Charles Lyell, a highly successful entrepreneur who built Kentucky's most celebrated spa, an authority on the early history of Kentucky, and, not least among his endless list of adventures and accomplishments, a crack rifleman widely celebrated as "the undisputed champion offhand rifle shot."

The Graham influence on William came both through his daughter Sarah Sutton Graham, who raised him, and of course through Dr. Graham himself, and his visit when William was eight.

1901

W.T.D. graduates and receives Doctor of Medicine from Columbian University Medical School. He had no money to go into private practice. He knew that his great grandfather and great-great-grandfather had served with distinction in the military* and was proud of this ancestral tradition. We believe this prompted him to pursue his medical career in the Army. Service in the military at that time was voluntary (no draft).

---

*W.T.D. was a member of the Society of the Cincinnati, an organization made up of descendants of officers of the Continental Army in the Revolutionary War. His great-great-grandfather James Graham (Dr. Graham's father) had served on the staff of George Rogers Clark in what was then the northwest frontier of the new nation.

OATH OF OFFICE.

One to accompany the acceptance of every commissioned officer appointed or commissioned by the President in the Army of the United States.

I, *Wm. T. Davis*, having been appointed a *1st Lieut. U.S. Army* in the military service of the United States, do solemnly swear (or affirm) that I will support and defend the Constitution of the United States against all enemies, foreign and domestic; that I will bear true faith and allegiance to the same; that I take this obligation freely, without any mental reservation or purpose of evasion; and that I will well and faithfully discharge the duties of the office on which I am about to enter. So help me God.

Wm. Thornwall Davis

Sworn to and subscribed before me, at *Washington DC*, this *9*ᵗʰ day of *July* 1902.

A. Greer

Notary Public

Oath of office sworn by W.T.D. on his appointment as 1st Lieutenant, U.S. Army Medical Corps.

APRIL 1902
He applied to Secretary of War for permission to appear before the Medical Examining Board for an Assistant Surgeonship in the U.S. Army Medical Corps.

JUNE 1902
He reported for his Army Medical Corps exam. These were very competitive examinations — he competed with Harvard and other top medical school graduates from around the country. His final exam was in written and oral form. Waiting in the outer office before his exam, he picked up a medical journal, read about a "rare disease," went into the oral exam and was asked about that same "rare disease." He said that "he lucked out a little because he had all the detail on it." He was selected from among many qualified applicants and received a commission. It was an honor to be selected as a medical officer in the service.

JULY 9, 1902
Oath of office and appointment to 1st Lieutenant, U.S. Army Medical Corps. (See W.T.D.'s Oath of Office document on facing page.)
   He interned at Garfield Memorial Hospital in Washington for one year.

1903
Graduated from Army Medical school (#10 out of 39).

JUNE 30, 1903, TO SEPTEMBER 2, 1904
Assistant Surgeon on the U.S. Army Transport *Logan* from San Francisco to Manila, the Philippines. A 1903 efficiency report on Dr. Davis by Major Ogden Rafferty, Medical Superintendent on the *Logan*, read "Duties performed in a very satisfactory manner. Habits, general conduct and bearing, and capacity for command, excellent. Condition and discipline of men, under his control, Good. Should be intrusted with important duties and is qualified for his position."
   Extract from a report by Col. W. S. McCaskey, commanding 20th Infantry troops on board: "The health of the command has been excellent and the medical department of the transport efficiently administered under Assistant Surgeon Davis, a most competent officer and gentlemanly associate."
   From a report by Major H. H. Benham, commanding 23rd Infantry: "Assistant Surgeon Davis, by his ability and unremitting attention day and

night, has carried through some very serious cases and by his watchfulness I believe has checked a large increase in the number of cases of pneumonia and measles."

As shown at left, W.T.D. was formally relieved from duty as surgeon on the *Logan*, on its arrival, in order to serve in the Philippines.

SEPTEMBER 2, 1904
W.T.D arrives in Manila during the Philippine Insurrection, also known as the Moro Rebellion.*

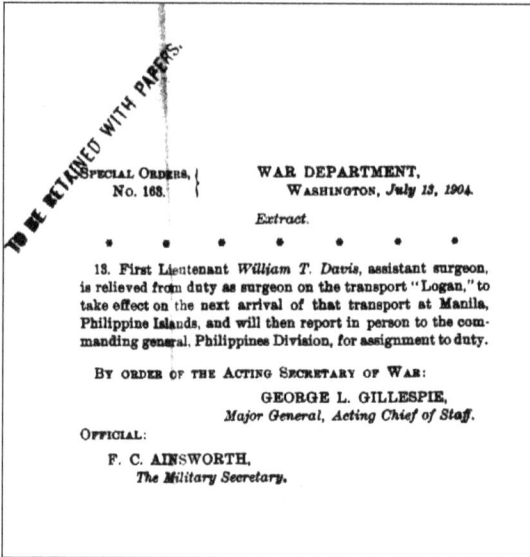

Order relieving W.T.D. from duty aboard the 'Logan' so that he could serve in the Philippines.

SEPTEMBER 2–NOVEMBER 10, 1904
Sanitary Inspector, Division Headquarters, Manila.

NOVEMBER 10, 1904, TO DECEMBER 2, 1905
Assistant Surgeon, Post Hospital, Zamboanga, Mindanao (second largest and southernmost major island in the Philippines).

One afternoon when a thunderstorm was forming he remembered that he hadn't closed the door to his quarters. In full uniform, he jumped on a horse and dashed back towards his quarters. He had to take the path down

---

*The Moro Rebellion (1899–1913) was an armed conflict between Moro indigenous ethnic groups and the U.S. military that took place on the islands of Mindanao, Sulu, and Palawan (Minsupala) in the Philippines but was not connected to the Spanish–American War (1898–1901). The Philippine Insurrection after the Spanish–American War was an uprising by the Moro natives from the hills and back country primarily on the island of Mindanao. The Moros were not "the small Filipinos as we know them" but a race of tall and large people of bravery and pride. A primary objective of the U.S. troops was to capture or kill Datu Ali, the leader of the Moros. Many military campaigns were carried out into the jungles and swamps to this end.

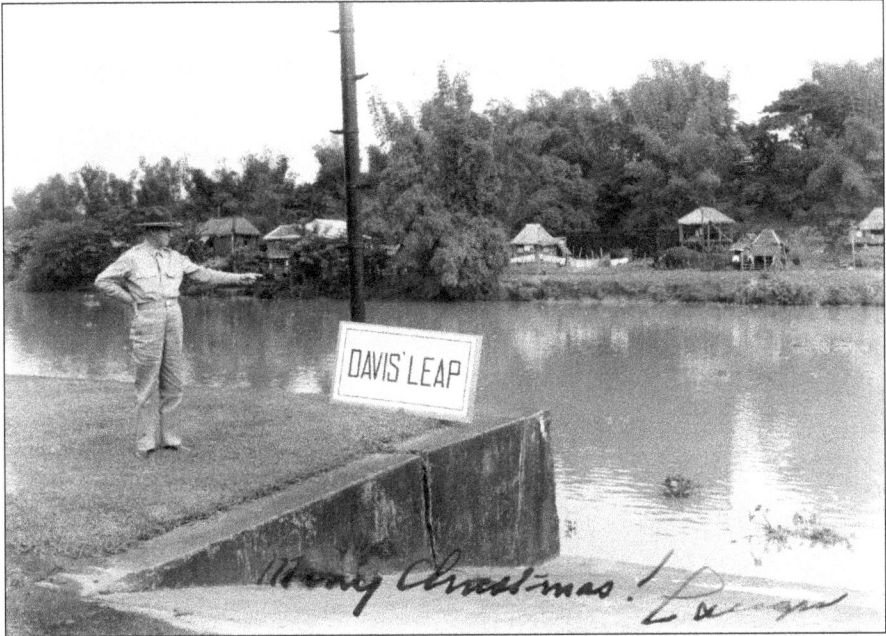

The site of W.T.D.'s unintentional ride into a lagoon at Zamboanga, The Philippines, an incident commemorated as "Davis's Leap."

toward a lagoon and make a sharp right to get to his quarters. His horse didn't know that, though, and they both went straight into the muddy lagoon. He had to pull himself and the horse out of the mud, go to his quarters, and put on a clean uniform. (A slightly different version of the "leap" is one recollected by Uncle Akin. W.T.D. was returning, after dark, to his quarters from the Officers Club, didn't see the lagoon and rode his horse into the water and mud.) Years later, W.T.D. told his sons he never knew anyone else had knowledge of that incident until an officer friend sent him a picture of the scene of "Davis's Leap." This photo hung on Dad's (Roger HB. Davis's) office wall.

1905

Report on W.T.D. from Major F. J. Ives, surgeon, commanding Military Hospital, Zamboanga: "Attention to duty, professional zeal, general bearing and military appearance, and intelligence and judgement shown in instructing, drilling, and handling enlisted men, Excellent." Report from

Col. J. T. VanOrsdale, 17th Infantry, commanding Zamboanga: "Has availed himself of his opportunities, is qualified for his position, should be intrusted with important duties, and in the event of war is best suited for his professional duties. He is very attentive to duties."

Following are a series of family stories and official reports about the campaigns against the Moros in which Lieutenant Davis participated:

DECEMBER 12–27, 1904
Dr. Davis was surgeon with expedition (two companies, 17th Infantry) against Moros. Proceeded across island of Mindanao. No engagement.

Campaign stories
W.T.D.'s company had stopped to camp in a small clearing. The soldiers had stacked their rifles in the middle of the clearing and while they were doing their chores a Moro ran out of the brush toward one of the soldiers swinging a tremendous kris (wavy sword) over his head (the Moro was between the man and the stacked rifles). The unarmed soldier stood transfixed looking at the Moro running at him. W.T.D., a medical officer, saw the Moro, drew his .45, knew he had time for only one shot, fired, and brought the Moro down at the feet of the defenseless soldier. (Grandpa's .45 was stolen from his closet shelf on Lowell Street years later.)

A soldier on one of these campaigns claimed to be friendly with the natives. He would sneak off at night to barter for fresh food (fruits and chickens, particularly). One morning it was reported that he did not return. He was found nearby staked to the ground, hacked to pieces.

There were times marching back to base camp that Lieutenant Davis would carry all of his medical supplies plus a couple of rifles belonging to 200-pound soldiers who were too fatigued to carry them. He was 5' 7" and 125–130 pounds.

After returning from a campaign, William, who was adjutant at the time, found an order from Headquarters calling for another campaign. He gave the orders to the commanding officer, who immediately issued a command for everyone to prepare for another expedition. Bedlam ensued until it was discovered that the "new" order was just a delayed copy of the order that had previously been sent for the campaign just completed. William was embarrassed, to say the least.

When Moros were taken as prisoners during campaigns they walked in front of Dr. Davis during marches and carried the U.S. wounded. His first responsibility during a Moro attack was "to get rid of those prisoners [terminate them]" because in a fight they would turn, attack, and kill the American wounded. Grandpa would not explain to his sons how he would do this and how often he had to do this. Dad can remember his mom telling her husband once, while he was telling this story, "Stop, don't go any further with your story."

Dr. Davis found that upon returning to base camp with wounded, those soldiers with maggots in their wounds would never have infection. He would take them to the shallow ocean surf and let the salt water cleanse their wounds. Years later modern hospitals learned to place maggots in dirty and infected wounds. The maggots would eat all the bad flesh and not touch the healthy flesh. Grandpa learned this before the hospitals began the practice.

Lieutenant Davis had considerable contact and communication with the Moro medicine men. He found them very intelligent and smart (that's why they became medicine men). These medicine men were interested in learning as much medical knowledge as they could from William, and in turn William learned much from them about their native medicines and treatments.

At some point in a later campaign, Lieutenant Davis's company of men traversed swampy and dense terrain to meet a supply boat on a river. They could only travel through these swamps with the help of loyal Philippine guides who knew how to wade through mud and hip-deep water and stay on firm ground, avoiding treacherous deep holes. It was Christmas Eve and the company was delayed. No food and raining. In his tent, William found a chocolate bar and one cigarette, which he divided with a friend for Christmas Eve dinner. Next afternoon, cloudy and rainy, they finally arrived at their boat, which was all prepared for a big Christmas dinner. A single plank board was placed on the bank to the boat for every soldier to walk. Food and drink were on board. The soldier, loaded with gear walking in front of William, when he saw the boat, the dry, covered deck, the Christmas food and drink, slipped and fell into the water. He was promptly eaten by crocodiles, there was no way to save him. He had been looking at the boat, not at the plank. Dad (Roger) said that when his father (Grandpa) told him this story in the 1930s there were tears in his eyes. "To come all of this way and to have this happen was a tragedy."

The story of "Battle-Axe Bob"

Bob Patterson, a fellow medical officer and close friend of Lieutenant Davis, was a large and powerful man who participated in numerous campaigns and many battles with these powerful natives. Often in close combat, after his ammunition was expended, he would turn his .38 revolver around, hold it by the barrel, and use it as a club. In one incident, he brought his revolver down on the head of an attacking Moro with such force that it came to rest between the man's shoulders. Thus, he earned the nickname, "Battle-Axe Bob."

He later became Surgeon General of the Army. After W.T.D. died, Bob Patterson came to Lowell Street (Grandpa's home in Washington) the next morning from Baltimore to extend his condolences. Bob's son, Bob Patterson, Jr., represented Dad as a financial advisor and often joined the Davis family at the annual Carabao Wallow in Washington, D.C.

OCTOBER 13–29, 1905 – DATU ALI EXPEDITION

Extract from report:

"Lieutenant Davis was surgeon with provisional company, 22nd Infantry on the Datu Ali Expedition in which there was an engagement at Malola River, October 22, 1905, in which Datu Ali and many of his men were killed."

In 1992 I, Robert Davis, wrote a full accounting of this remarkable military campaign, which I titled *The Quest for Datu Ali*. Much of the background information for this story came from a very long article in the Chicago *Sunday Tribune* dated September 6, 1936, and found by my father in the Library of Congress. This is an extraordinary family story for present and future generations.

THE QUEST FOR DATU ALI

Compiled by Robert G. Davis (age 47), November 1992. Read to the Davis family in Charlottesville, Virginia, Christmas 1992, by Robert Davis in honor of my grandfather, William T. Davis, and my father, Roger HB. Davis, one of his four sons. Roger HB. Davis (age 75) and Geraldine H. Davis (age 65) were present.

FIRST PART: THE DURIAN TREE

Ferdinand Magellan, who led the first expedition that sailed around the world, was not to live to complete his historic voyage, for when he landed in the Philippines, he was killed in a battle with the natives. This is when our story begins, almost 500 years ago, in April, 1521, when the Spaniards first landed on the islands of the Philippines.

The Spaniards found the natives to be small in stature, dark-haired and dark-skinned. They had formed many small communities throughout the islands, and each group had developed its own culture. The Spaniards found one type of native far different than the others. These natives were more intelligent, much larger in stature and much stronger; they were more cunning, more aggressive and more violent; they were proud, fearless men and women who took what they wanted and what they needed — their ancestors were Mohammedans who had come by sea from Malaysia — they had brought the faith of Islam with them. The Spaniards called them "MOROS."

The Moros had their own nobility who were believed to have true Arabic blood in their veins. These noblemen were called Datus. These Datus often became rulers of the districts in which they dwelt. They were then referred to as sultans, and, as followers of the prophet Mohammed, they maintained harems. In all of the 7,000 islands of the Philippines there were no warriors more feared than the Moros, and no Moros more difficult to combat than their noblemen, the Datus.

The favorite arm of the Moros was the kris — a wicked, swordlike cutting weapon, some straight, some curved and wavy. Also used were spears, as well as firearms stolen from the white man.

The Spaniards, in 400 years of ruling the Philippines, were never really able to civilize and control the Moros of the large lower island of the Philippines, Mindanao. The Spaniards didn't try to govern the Moros on this lower island, only protect their forts and the other Filipinos on the island. In the 1890's the Filipinos began to seek political and social freedom from Spain. Freedom movements and revolts were organized.

In 1898, the United States and Spain fought over the independence of Cuba. During the war, the Americans also fought the Spaniards in the Philippines. Emilio Aguinaldo, leader of the Filipino revolutionary army, helped the Americans defeat the Spaniards. The Spanish-American War of 1898 was won rather quickly by the U.S. and marked the emergence of the U.S. as a world power. Through a peace treaty with Spain the U.S. gained possession of Guam, Puerto Rico, and the Philippines. Aguinaldo claimed that the U.S. had promised to make the Philippines independent immediately. He declared war on the Americans in 1899. After a two-year war, the U.S. captured Aguinaldo in 1901, and the fighting soon ended.

The fighting with the revolting Aguinaldo forces had basically taken place on the islands to the north and east of Mindanao. The last of the defeated Spaniards moved out of Mindanao in 1901 and there was a short period of time between the evacuation of the Spaniards and the arrival of the Americans.

This is when our story really begins. At this time the Moro sultan of the Rio Grande valley of Mindanao was Datu Ali, the most dangerous, the most ruthless, and the most powerful Sultan of all of Mindanao — he was a raider, a robber and a woman stealer. His territory was a great sprawling fertile lowland, crossed by streams, dotted by rice fields and surrounded by mountains, at the bases of which were dense, tropical jungles. He was a giant of a man, well over 6 feet in height. He was a fearless warrior and was equally proficient with the straight-bladed and the wavy kris. He and his followers moved down the Rio Grande and raided the town of Cotabato. They looted native homes and slashed and killed natives with their krises. The ground became blood red. Datu Ali then ordered all of the women paraded in front of him and he picked those who he fancied the most. They feasted and caroused. When the Americans finally arrived, Datu Ali, his wives, children and his followers vanished into the wilds of the upper Rio Grande valley.

In 1902, after much effort to pacify the Moros and start friendly relations with Datu Ali, the American commander of the Mindanao region invited Datu Ali and his wives along with other groups of Filipinos to the Louisiana Purchase exposition in St. Louis. At the last moment, after learning that the Moros were slave owners and that some of Ali's party were slaves, the American government called off the invitation. This was an insult to the proud Moro chief. He had lost face with his own people. He broke off relations with the Americans for good.

Shortly thereafter, the Americans bombarded the Moro fort at Serenaya and drove out Ali and 1,200–2,000 of his followers — a two-year war with Ali began.

Ali and his warriors were shrewd and slippery. They would raid throughout the valley of the Rio Grande and ambush American detachments — then would vanish like the wind into the jungles. Peaceful natives were afraid to betray him, for his vengeance was far reaching. He would even raid beyond the limits of his territory. He looted villages, put to death those who opposed him, and stole all the pretty women that he fancied.

After one very bloody ambush of Americans in which 22 soldiers were slain, Captain McCoy, a young American officer active in the campaign with the Moros, was ordered up into the hills to warn peaceful natives about Ali. In his small party of soldiers and natives was Datu Enok, a foster brother of Datu Ali, who went along as a guide. Enok was Ali's mortal enemy for Ali had stolen Enok's favorite wife, Makalle. McCoy and his men were the first Americans to ever penetrate the isolated regions of the center of Mindanao (south of Mt. Apo, the highest peak in the Philippines). One evening during the expedition, while camping near Buluan on the Malala River, Enok and McCoy stood together on the Malala riverbank and gazed at the colorful panorama. Enok pointed to a great pyramidal tree to the northeast that reared above the surrounding landscape and said, "That's a durian tree, it's the only one within a hundred miles. Natives come here from over the whole valley to eat of its fruit." The durian tree bears a spherical fruit 6-8" in diameter, with a hard prickly rind. And, when ripe, the inside has the consistency of custard. Although it had an offensive smell ("smelled to the heavens," as McCoy said), the natives liked it.

For months thereafter, Ali's defiance continued. There was one more attempt to arrange a truce with the wily Moro sultan. American officers met with Ali at the ranch of Datu Piang, a cunning old chieftain, part Moro and part Chinese. After days of talks, Datu Ali agreed to terms and to a surrender of arms. But, just before the surrender, the shrewd old sultan, who had been fooling all along, vanished into the night, taking with him Datu Piang's favorite daughter, the beautiful Princess Minka.

Captain McCoy, acting governor of Mindanao at that time, and his staff were stationed in Zamboanga. After much discussion they decided to make one more try for the slippery Ali. They went back to Datu Piang to see what they could learn about Ali's whereabouts. Piang was friendly to the Americans but also fearful of the vengeance of Ali. He wanted to appear to cooperate with McCoy, but he did not want to tell him exactly where Ali was hiding. McCoy pushed and pushed for information. McCoy was getting nowhere. But, just about the time McCoy was giving up hope, Piang told him that a couple of weeks before, Ali had sent for Minka's mother to nurse Minka through a spell of sickness. The old woman had been taken way up the river and through the swamps to the Malala River. She had returned to Piang's place just the day before McCoy's arrival. Piang told McCoy that Ali was hiding on the Malala River. Piang knew that there were literally thousands of places to hide along the river, so he knew he wasn't letting on to Ali's location. The old native told McCoy that Ali was staying in a house on high ground somewhere on the banks of the Malala. Then, without giving the matter a thought, Piang said that the house stood under a durian tree.

That was enough for Captain McCoy. That was the key.

SECOND PART: GRANDFATHER DAVIS AND THE GOLDEN RING
Back to Zamboanga went McCoy. It was decided that McCoy would lead an expedition at once to capture or kill Datu Ali. It would be a secret expedition since news of what the Americans were doing traveled fast through the Moros. The expedition would take a different route than any they had taken before. They would sail to Davao Gulf and march overland to the Malala River from the south. A march from the north would have no secrecy — Ali would know far in advance of the raid. By going in the back door, so to speak, McCoy would have a chance to trap the foxy old chief.

This route, though, was through the rankest kind of jungles and swamps, over a divide and along the base of the mountains. (See next page for map of Mindanao and expedition route.)

To maintain the strictest secrecy, McCoy selected soldiers for his expedition from the camp most remote from the valley of the Rio Grande. A company of the 22nd Infantry, stationed at Camp Keithly on Lake L'anao. The soldiers were swiftly brought to Zamboanga under the pretense of undertaking an expedition to the Sulu Islands.

There were 100 soldiers and about 150 native bearers and scouts. Among those selected were Datu Enok, the sworn enemy of Ali, and Tomas Torres, a Filipino veteran of Moro wars, whose wife had also been stolen by Ali. Torres knew Ali by sight. The lone doctor on the expedition was Grandfather, 27-year-old Dr. William T. Davis. The soldiers were armed with Springfields, a magazine-fed breech loading, bolt-action .30 caliber rifle, later used by the U.S. in WWI. But McCoy and his officers felt that their sidearm pistols were inadequate. They communicated back to Washington that they needed more powerful handguns, because, when you shot one of these big Moros with their regulation .32 caliber revolvers, the Moro would just keep on coming swinging his kris. And, so powerful were these Moros and their deadly krises that a man could be cut in two. So this small but very important company of soldiers were among the first to be issued the heavier .45 caliber pistol, in the knowledge that the Moros "required a weight of lead to stop them." Dr. Davis carried only a sidearm (a .45 caliber pistol) because of all the other heavy medical gear he had to haul. Also, some of the men were issued a new color of khaki shirt (light brown). Dr. Davis wore one of these shirts.

The expedition sailed from Zamboanga to Davao Gulf. The plan was to push forward over land as fast as possible to reach the house under the durian tree before Ali learned of the advance. They plunged into the jungle. The advance took six days, they marched primarily by night, sweating and struggling through the swamps, jungles and other treacherous terrain. Approximately 30 of the American soldiers were overcome by fatigue along the way, and, since there could be no delays in their mission, they had to be left behind at various points.

Dr. Davis was a fit young man of great endurance and courage, weighing only about 130 pounds. He had to carry his heavy medical gear but still found the strength to help his bigger and stronger comrades who struggled

Dr. William Thornwall Davis Ophthalmologist, Wash., D. C. a. 1942

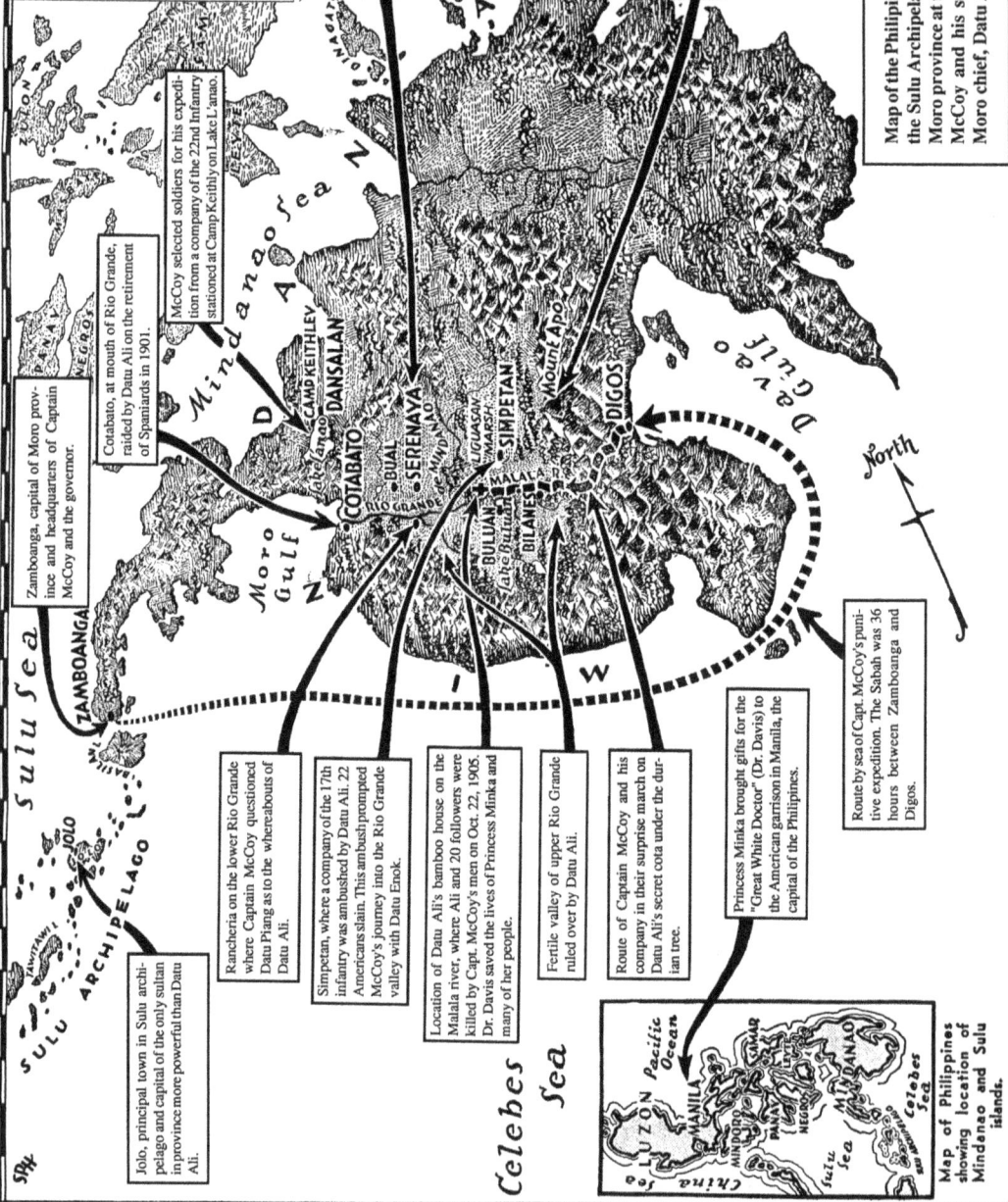

Map of the Philipine island of Mindanao and the Sulu Archipelago, which constituted the Moro province at the time Captain Frank R. McCoy and his soldiers put an end to the Moro chief, Datu Ali.

Cota at Serenaya occupied by Datu Ali and 1,200 to 2,000 followers. Moros driven out by bombardment of Wood's artillery. This marked the beginning of a two year war with the Moros.

Mount Apo (9,610 feet high), tallest peak in the Philipines.

Pacific Ocean

Mindanao Sea

M I N D A N A O

CAMP KEITHLEY
DANSALAN
COTABATO
BUAL
SERENAYA
Lake Lanao
SIMPETAN
LIGUASAY MARSH
Mount Apo
DIGOS
Davao Gulf
BULUAN
Lake Buluan
MALALA
BILANES
RIO GRANDE

Moro Gulf

ZAMBOANGA

Sulu Sea

JOLO
TAWITAWI
SULU ARCHIPELAGO

McCoy selected soldiers for his expedition from a company of the 22nd Infantry stationed at Camp Keithly on Lake L'anao.

Cotabato, at mouth of Rio Grande, raided by Datu Ali on the retirement of Spaniards in 1901.

Zamboanga, capital of Moro province and headquarters of Captain McCoy and the governor.

Jolo, principal town in Sulu archipelago and capital of the only sultan in province more powerful than Datu Ali.

Rancheria on the lower Rio Grande where Captain McCoy questioned Datu Piang as to the whereabouts of Datu Ali.

Simpetan, where a company of the 17th infantry was ambushed by Datu Ali. 22 Americans slain. This ambush prompted McCoy's journey into the Rio Grande valley with Datu Enok.

Location of Datu Ali's bamboo house on the Malala river, where Ali and 20 followers were killed by Capt. McCoy's men on Oct. 22, 1905. Dr. Davis saved the lives of Princess Minka and many of her people.

Fertile valley of upper Rio Grande ruled over by Datu Ali.

Route of Captain McCoy and his company in their surprise march on Datu Ali's secret cota under the durian tree.

Princess Minka brought gifts for the "Great White Doctor" (Dr. Davis) to the American garrison in Manila, the capital of the Philippines.

Route by sea of Capt. McCoy's punitive expedition. The Sabah was 36 hours between Zamboanga and Digos.

North

Celebes Sea

LUZON
MINDORO
SAMAR
PANAY
NEGROS
MINDANAO
MANILA
Pacific Ocean
China Sea
Sulu Sea
Celebes Sea

Map of Philippines showing location of Mindanao and Sulu islands.

with exhaustion. He would often carry equipment belonging to other soldiers so they could keep pace with the advancing column.

When they found those precious hours to sleep, Dr. Davis, as he used to say to his children, "would sleep with one eye open and a revolver in his hand." The Moros were expert at creeping up on unsuspecting American soldiers. Once, on a previous expedition, sleeping in a hut with thatch floors raised high above ground, Dr. Davis woke up suddenly to a piercing and horrible screaming. A Moro had sneaked into camp, crawled under the hut, and jammed a spear up into the floor and straight through the chest of a soldier sleeping next to Dr. Davis. The Moro then disappeared into the jungle night.

In the early daylight hours of the sixth morning, the advancing column came to the banks of the Malala River. The native bearers at this point were left behind. Haste and surprise were all important. The Americans and a few scouts advanced rapidly, crossing and recrossing the river several times until they came to the ford nearest the house under the durian tree. It was sheer luck that the guard of seven Moros watching the crossing had departed for breakfast shortly before the weary American soldiers arrived at approximately 6:00 A.M.

A small group of 17 picked men was ordered to go forward through the tall grasses as speedily as possible to capture or kill Datu Ali before the Moros could organize resistance. Datu Enok, Tom Torres and Dr. Davis were among the 17. They advanced at a dog trot through the tall grasses. Another platoon moved to the left to cover the river. And another platoon proceeded to the right to keep any of the enemy from fleeing on that side by way of the river.

McCoy and the remaining soldiers had stayed behind to wait for the returning guards. Suddenly, above the waving tall grass, they saw the bouncing spears of the seven Moro guards who were returning from their morning coffee. They wanted to take the seven without sounding the alarm and warning Ali. Just as they pounced on the natives the sounds of gunfire came from the vicinity of Datu Ali's bamboo hideout. They rushed towards the house.

The small group of 17 men who had gone forward to take Ali had, again by luck, been able to avoid the seven returning guards. Near the house there was a narrow path through the tall grass through which the soldiers had to move single file. When the point men emerged from the grass into the small clearing in front of the bamboo house, they saw a group of Moros on the front porch. The Moros retreated into the house and lay on the floor firing through the cracks of the bamboo. The soldiers, as they reached the clearing, started firing and filed alternately left and right to take cover. The man in front of Dr. Davis went to the right as Dr. Davis then went to the left — at that point the man to the right was shot through the heart and crumpled dead to the ground, he had been wearing one of the same newly issued light brown shirts as Dr. Davis — Dr. Davis heard the man behind him say, "Oh, my God, they got the Doc!"

The battle had begun. The Americans let loose with a barrage of bullets into the bamboo fortress. Suddenly, a gigantic Moro emerged from the door of the house — his gleaming body nude except for a scanty breech-cloth. In his hands was a Mauser rifle, the bolt of which he was working furiously as he fast delivered a stream of bullets toward the line of soldiers before him. He killed one of the soldiers. More than a dozen American soldiers let loose their Springfields at the man. Every bullet hit him. He fell. "That was Ali!" shouted Tomas Torres.

After an additional barrage, Datu Enok called to those in the house to surrender. To the surprise of the soldiers, a woman's voice answered that all of the men had been killed. There had been 21 Moro men in the house, some had fled into the jungle, and only Ali had stood up to fight it out with his enemies. But, to the shock of the Americans, there were 20 women and children also in the house. Nearly all of them lying on the floor wounded and dying. The Moros, by tradition when under attack, would protect their women and children by placing them in the center of their fort or house. The Americans had no idea that they were firing into such a situation and that their bullets were ricocheting off the thick, hard bamboo into the mass of women and children huddled inside.

A woman, stark naked, walked out of the house. In her arms she held a baby — she was badly wounded. She was Datu Enok's stolen wife, Makalle.

Dr. Davis immediately attended to the wounds of the women and children, as well as those of the Americans, two of whom had been killed and three wounded. Some of the wounded in the house he could help, others were so badly wounded he couldn't do much.

One of the wounded in the house was a beautiful young Moro woman. Dr. Davis knew that she must have been someone special because she was dressed in fine clothing and wore beautiful jewels. Barely conscious, she was bleeding to death from a bullet wound which had ripped and opened up her arm from wrist to shoulder; fortunately, it did not rupture any major arteries. She resisted Dr. Davis and at first would not let him dress her wounds. This was the Princess Minka. As royalty, she was among the proudest of the Moros. She had been taught by the Moro medicine men not to accept medicine from the white man and that their bandages were unclean. After urging from Captain McCoy and Dr. Davis, Minka finally accepted care. Dr. Davis managed to stop the bleeding, served the wound, and carefully bandaged her arm. Minka was unconscious when the Doctor finished dressing her wounds. He put her bandaged arm in a sling, tied her other arm behind her, and then tied her loosely to a nearby post, in hopes that when she regained consciousness she would not rip the bandages from her arm.

Dr. Davis did the best he could with the other wounded in the short time he had. The small force of soldiers had to move quickly and get out of there because there were many more Moros in the area. They went northeast, by way of the upper Rio Grande valley, and back to Zamboanga.

Weeks later, Datu Piang asked Captain McCoy, "What was Datu Ali wearing when he was killed?"

"Only a breechcloth," McCoy said.

"Didn't he have on a shirt?", said the old man.

"No," said McCoy.

"Then that's why he was killed. He wasn't wearing his magic shirt," confided Piang.

It seems that Ali, as an alleged descendant of Mohammed, possessed a bulletproof shirt of silk, and a pot of sacred oil that was guaranteed to keep him safe from harm. But, no charms were working that day on the banks of the Malala River when he stopped more than a dozen bullets. From the day of that last battle, October 22, 1905, there was a lasting peace in the valley of the Rio Grande and on the island of Mindanao.

But this is not the end of our story. Months afterward, a strange and unexpected thing happened. While Dr. Davis was stationed in Manila, capital of the Philippines, a beautiful young Moro woman walked into the American garrison; she had a badly scarred arm. She asked that her gold ring and a Moro sword, inlaid with rubies and emeralds, be given to the "great white doctor" who had saved her life and the lives of many of her people. She then quickly left and returned to the jungle. This, of course, had been the Princess Minka.

Grandfather Davis shipped the sword and other memorabilia back to the U. S.. They were lost or destroyed in the great San Francisco earthquake and fire of 1906, one of the worst disasters in U.S. history, which left most of San Francisco in ruins and killed approximately 700 people. The ring? Dr. Davis carried it with him on his return to the United States. The Davis family will continue to pass it on to future generations as a symbol of the courageous spirit and compassion of our Grandfather Davis.

END

PHOTO: MONICA PEDYNKOWSKI

OCTOBER 31, 1905
Letter from Captain McCoy, organizer and leader of the Datu Ali Expedition, recommending Philippine decoration be given to his men (see following page). The ribbon was never given.

DECEMBER 6, 1905
Lieutenant Davis relieved from his duty in the Philippines Division with special orders for a three-month leave of absence. He had permission to return to the U.S. via the Suez Canal but was free to choose his own itinerary en route. He decided to travel, alone, through China to India.

Before he left the Philippines he shipped the Moro kris given to him by the princess, and all other memorabilia, except the ring, to San Francisco. As noted, they were lost or destroyed in the April 18, 1906 Great San Francisco Earthquake. During the fires in San Francisco one of William's doctor friends was trying to aid an injured person. U.S. soldiers who had been ordered to fire on looters called to him to stop. He did not hear the soldiers' command and was shot dead.

DECEMBER 15, 1905, TO APRIL 7, 1906
Travel through China and India to the Suez Canal and back to the U.S.. While traveling through China as a U.S. officer (there were no hotels then) he was often invited to stay with wealthy families in the community. It was the Chinese custom at that time to have the best daughter spend the night with the honored guest. Grandpa told his sons that he "felt a little awkward but what could a young man do?" While in Shanghai and formally dressed for a social function he chose to go by rickshaw, a small, two-wheeled carriage pulled along by one person. He soon realized that he was being led in the wrong direction through some back streets and alleys so he called out to the rickshaw driver, "I want to go that way." At that moment the rickshaw runner stopped, drew back over his head a large kris, and with great force brought it down over Grandpa's head. But the tip of the sword caught in the top canvas and rigging of the rickshaw, Grandpa pulled his .45 and shot the man twice through the head. He jumped out and ran away. (Another version of this incident from Uncle Akin has the attack occurring in the Philippines.)

When he reached India he had no way of getting across the country to Bombay except by ship around the horn of India (there was no commercial transportation). However, he met some British officers in Calcutta

HEADQUARTERS DEPARTMENT OF MINDANAO,

Zamboanga, P. I. .

October 31st, 1905.

Military Secretary
    Department of Mindanao,
        Zamboanga, P. I.

Sir:
    I have the honor to submit the following report on
the Datu Ali Expedition.

    1st Lieut. W. T. Davis, Assistant Surgeon, U. S. A.

The conduct of this picked body of officers and men
was excellent throughout. I have the honor to recommend that
they be entitled to wear the official decoration for Moro
Campaigns, which is limited in time to Dec. 31st, last, or
that a special ribbon be authorized for this successful expedition; that acknowledgement be made in orders of the War
Department --.

Very respectfully.
    F. R. McCOY.
        Captain, 3rd Cavalry. A. D. C. .
            Commanding.

To The Military Secretary
    of the Army,

For file with Lieutenant Davis' record.

S. G. C. .
  Feb. 1, 1906.

*Recommendation for an exception in the case of W.T.D. and others
from the Datu Ali expedition, so that they could be awarded the official
ribbon for Moro Campaigns.*

who were involved in a campaign to march across India to Bombay, and they invited him along. He at first declined because he was a U.S. officer in uniform, but they said not to worry, they would provide him with a British uniform, so off they went. Grandpa told Dad many stories about his trip across India. They visited with maharajahs (Indian princes or kings ranking above the rajahs) and went on tiger hunts on the backs of elephants.

April 7–21, 1906
Duty with Company A, Hospital Corps, Washington Barracks, Washington, D.C.

April 21–June 21, 1906
Duty with Field Hospital in Golden Gate Park, San Francisco. Relief help to sufferers from the earthquake and fire of April 18.

From MILITARY SURGEON, Vol. 19, No. 1 (July 1906)*
EDITORIAL EXPRESSION
THE WORK OF THE MEDICAL DEPARTMENT OF THE
UNITED STATES ARMY AT SAN FRANCISCO

We find in the *Army and Navy Register* for June 9th so interesting a note upon the work of the Army Medical Department, in connection with the San Francisco catastrophe, that we reproduce it, together with the illustrations kindly loaned us for the purpose. The *Register* remarks that:

"On the day in which the news of the disaster reached Washington, that is to say a few hours after the breaking out of the big fire on the morning of the earthquake, the surgeon general of the Army took steps to have shipped from St. Louis to San Francisco a trainload of medical and surgical supplies. The medical officers on the ground at once applied themselves the arduous task of establishing temporary hospitals and arranging for the treatment of those who were injured, as well as those who were sick. It is one thing to establish and maintain a field hospital even in time of war, and it is quite another thing to establish hospitals in a stricken city. In the former case the medical officers are prepared for the work and its emergency. In the latter case there can be no such preliminary work. The general sani-

*Special thanks to Christopher Davis, one of Uncle Akin's three sons, for finding and sharing this article through his searches on the internet.

Medical officers and noncommissioned officers of Company A, Hospital Corps, at Golden Gate Park Field Hospital. Lieutenant Davis seated at right.

tary situation was in charge of Lieutenant Colonel George H. Torney of the medical department, who worked faithfully and well until relieved of the duty by General Greely, who transferred the duty to civilian authorities.

"A branch of the medical work which has been done in San Francisco in the Golden Gate Park Field Hospital, in charge of Captain H. L. Gilchrist, who has associated with him in this work **Lieutenant William T. Davis**, of the medical department. **The field hospital was erected and maintained by the members of Company A of the hospital corps**, which left Washington on April 21, under command of Captain Gilchrist. Orders were received one morning for the departure of the company for San Francisco, and by afternoon the company was ready to go on board the train. This incident showed what could be done in the medical department to meet an unexpected call for duty at a distant place. The command, went fully equipped in all respects, and on arrival in San Francisco proceeded to the work of establishing a field hospital which was located at Golden Gate Park.

"In this institution is an isolation hospital, established in anticipation

General view of Golden Gate Park Field Hospital.

of a typhoid epidemic in the large colony of refugees, but there have been only two cases of typhoid, owing to the maintenance of excellent sanitary conditions. According to the latest reports, there were 130 patients in the field tents, including some emergency cases and others of longer duration.

"Observers who have no connection with the Army and who have excellent opportunities of seeing what is going on in San Francisco unite in praising the Army medical officers and the hospital corps men for their excellent work. They accomplish much more than would be done by the civilian inspectors from the municipal health department, and it is a question whether the civilian authorities will exact the same observation of the rules for the preservation of health which have been adopted and enforced by the Army medical officers. A part of the problem which confronts the health board in San Francisco is the housing of the refugees during the next year. It will probably be at least twelve months before all of them are in homes of their own and in the meantime there must be, it is held, some way of quartering many families which are now living in tents. This may be done by means of three room buildings erected on city land and rented at the rate of $3 per month. A community which lives in this fashion, will have to observe sanitary conditions with great care.

"Two interesting pictures are printed in this issue. One gives a general view of the Golden Gate Park Field Hospital under Captain Gilchrist. Up to May 19 there had been 500 patients received and at that time there were as many as 300 people receiving daily treatment at the free dispensary connected with the hospital. The rough sign attached to the tent bears the legend, "U. S. Army Golden Gate Park Field Hospital, Free Treatment to All." The general view of the camp gives an idea of its extent and arrangement."

JUNE 21–30, 1906
Back to Company A, Washington, D.C.

JULY 1–SEPTEMBER 16, 1906
Duty at Field Hospital #10, Chickamauga Park, Georgia.

SEPTEMBER 17–OCTOBER 2, 1906
Back to Company A, Washington, D.C.

OCTOBER 3–10, 1906
Duty with Company A, Washington, D.C., and Ambulance Company #2, Camp Newport News, Virginia.

OCTOBER 10–13, 1906
En route to Havana, Cuba.

OCTOBER 13, 1906 TO APRIL 15, 1907
Duty with Company A, Hospital Corps at Base Hospital, Army of Cuban Pacification, Havana, Cuba.

APRIL 15–MAY 7, 1907
Returns to Washington to take examination for promotion to Captain.

MAY 7–JUNE 25, 1907
Return to duty with Company A, Hospital Corps at Base Hospital, Havana, Cuba.

OATH OF OFFICE.

One to accompany the acceptance of every commissioned officer appointed or commissioned by the President in the Army of the United States.

I, *William T. Davis*, having been appointed a *Captain Medical Corps* in the military service of the United States, do solemnly swear (or affirm) that I will support and defend the Constitution of the United States against all enemies, foreign and domestic; that I will bear true faith and allegiance to the same; that I take this obligation freely, without any mental reservation or purpose of evasion; and that I will well and faithfully discharge the duties of the office on which I am about to enter: So help me God.

Sworn to and subscribed before me, at _____, this *16* day of *May* *1908*

FORM No. 337. A. G. O.

Oath of office sworn by W.T.D. on his appointment as Captain, U.S. Army Medical Corps.

W.T.D. standing (TOP ROW, FOURTH FROM LEFT) with his company of 81 men at Camp Columbia, Cuba. See pages 96–97 for entire photo..

MAY 8, 1908
W.T.D. was appointed Captain, Medical Corps, U.S. Army.

JULY 1, 1907 TO JANUARY 25, 1909
Duty with Army of Cuban Pacification* at Camp Columbia, Havana, Cuba.

W.T.D. had his first attack of acute dysentery in 1908 and had recurring

---

*The Second Occupation of Cuba by United States military forces, also known as the Cuban Pacification, lasted from September 1906 to February 1909. When the government of Cuban President Tomás Estrada Palma collapsed, U.S. President Theodore Roosevelt ordered U.S. military forces into Cuba. Their mission was to prevent fighting between the Cubans, to protect U.S. economic interests there, and to hold free elections in order to establish a new and legitimate government. Following the election of José Miguel Gómez in November 1908, U.S. officials judged the situation in Cuba sufficiently stable for the U.S. to withdraw its troops, a process that was completed in February 1909. An earlier occupation lasted from 1898–1902, from the conclusion of peace between the United States and Spain at the end of the Spanish–American War until the inauguration of the Republic of Cuba. (Source: Wikipedia)

Captain Davis in full uniform, 1909.

Renée Tolson at age three. Boys in foreground identified as "Don Seibert, Roy Seibert, Stanley Vail."

attacks in later years.

During this period in Havana, Grandpa met his wife to be, Renée Tolson (1887–1968), at a dance/reception at the U.S. Embassy. Renée was traveling with her guardian, Anginette Moyle HasBrouck, later known to Grandpa's four sons as Aunt Nettie. Anginette HasBrouck was well enough known and high enough in society that she and her daughter were invited to the reception where she met her future husband. Not much is known about Renée's background; what follows is what we have pieced together.

Renée's mother, Mary Rogers, lived in California and had married a Mr. Wilbur Tolson (originally from Washington, D.C.). Renée was born in a Sierra Nevada gold mining camp in 1887. Her mother died shortly thereafter, Mr. Tolson put her in an orphanage, and disappeared. Anginette HasBrouck and her husband wanted to adopt a little girl, visited the orphanage, and adopted Renée. They raised Renée as their child. Dad (Roger) had a copy of Anginette HasBrouck's will, which indicated that

Renée Tolson, age 16.

Near San Francisco: Renée third from left, and Anginette HasBrouck (Aunt Nettie) second from right.

Anginette HasBrouck's home on Pacific Avenue, San Francisco.

Renée Tolson in her early 20s.

Another view of the HasBrouck home.

HasBrouck home interior. The table in the foreground now sits in Uncle Akin's living room, at 3941 Legation Street, N.W., Washington, D.C. The chair to the right in the hallway can be found in the foyer of my Charlottesville, Virginia, home.

Anginette Moyle HasBrouck.

Renée on horseback.

they never formally adopted her. In the will Anginette referred to Renée as "her friend, Renée Tolson." They never changed her name. Mr. HasBrouck was successful in the real estate business in San Francisco. After he died, Anginette lived in San Francisco with Renée and lived off the income from numerous leased properties. Anginette, and her unmarried sister, Alice Moyle, raised Renée, educated her well, and traveled extensively with her to Europe (in 1906) and other places. Renée studied music in New York City and studied voice in Europe. Anginette died in the 1930s but Roger remembers visiting her in California when he was about 14 years old.

Meanwhile, all efficiency reports on William in Cuba commended his exemplary professionalism, attention to detail, perseverance, energy, intelligence, and judgment. We never found a report that was anything but complimentary before, during, or after this period.

JANUARY 27, 1909
Returned to U.S. as Assistant, Office of Attending Surgeon, Washington, D.C.

SUMMARY OF EFFICIENCY REPORTS.

Davis, William T.

1907. By Major C. Willcox, Surgeon U.S.A. commanding Base Hospital, Camp Columbia, Cuba. Attention to duty, professional zeal, general bearing and military appearance, intelligence and judgment shown in instructing, drilling and handling enlisted men, Excellent. Has shown no peculiar fitness for detail. He has availed himself of his opportunities for improvement, is qualified thoroughly for the duties of his position and should be intrusted with important ones requiring discretion and judgment. I consider him a most valuable man. Is well fitted for command of troops. . In the event of war would be an excellent man in the field, would also be valuable in any professional duty.

1908. By Major Charles Willcox, Medical-Corps, commanding Hospital, Camp Columbia, Cuba. Attention to duty, professional zeal, general bearing and military appearance, excellent. Intelligence and judgment shown in instructing, drilling, and handling enlisted men, very good. He has shown peculiar fitness for detail on the General Staff, as an instructor at the Military Academy or service schools in Hygiene. By character, disposition and ability would do well on recruiting, college, or militia duty. Working knowledge of Spanish and German. Has most thoroughly availed himself of his opportunities. Is thoroughly qualified for his position and should be intrusted with important duties requiring discretion and judgment. I would like very much to have him under my immediate command, in the event of war is suited for any work in field or hospital. A thoroughly well equipped medical officer, energetic and of good judgment.

1909. By Lieutenant Colonel G. L. Edie, Medical Corps, Attending Surgeon, Washington, D. C. Attention to duty, professional zeal, General bearing and military appearance, Excellent. Reads German and Spanish. Has availed himself of his opportunities for improvement professionally, is qualified for his position and should be intrusted with important duties.

1910. By Lieutenant Colonel Guy L. Edie, Medical Corps, Attending Surgeon, Washington, D.C. Under my observation from June 30, 1909 to July 1, 1910. Attention to duty, professional zeal, and general bearing and military appearance, excellent. Has availed himself of his opportunities for improvement professionally. Is qualified for his position and should be intrusted with important duties. In event of war is best suited for the duties of a medical officer. This officer has been most zealous in his efforts to perfect himself in his profession. His unremitting and faithful attention to his duties, his tact and skill in the performance of those duties, merits commendation and reflects credit upon himself and the service.

1911. By Major Matthew A. De Laney, Medical Corps, Attending Surgeon, Washington, D. C. Under my observation from July 1?, to December 31, 1911. Attention to duty, professional zeal and general bearing and military appearance, Excellent. Has availed himself of opportunities to improve himself professionally. No opportunity afforded to form an opinion as to his fitness to command troops. Qualified mentally, morally and physically for all his duties. desire to testify to the capable, thorough and efficient manner in which Captain Davis has performed his duties at this office while under my observation. Should be intrusted with important duties. In event of war is best fitted for Medical, Surgical, Ophthalmalogy and Optometry.

1912. By Major Matthew A. De Laney, Medical Corps, Attending Surgeon, Washington, D. C. Stationed at Washington, D. C., from January 1 to December 31, 1912. Attention to duty, professional zeal, general bearing and military appearance, and intelligence and judgment shown in instructing, drilling and handling enlisted men, excellent. Has shown peculiar fitness for detail on the General Staff, and might be detailed on recruiting, college and militia duty. Has availed himself of his opportunities for improvement, is an industrious and able officer. Is competent to command troops. Is qualified for his position and should be intrusted with important duties. Would be glad to have his services in peace or in war. In the event of war is best suited for duty in the medico-military.

Efficiency reports on William T. Davis, 1907-1912.

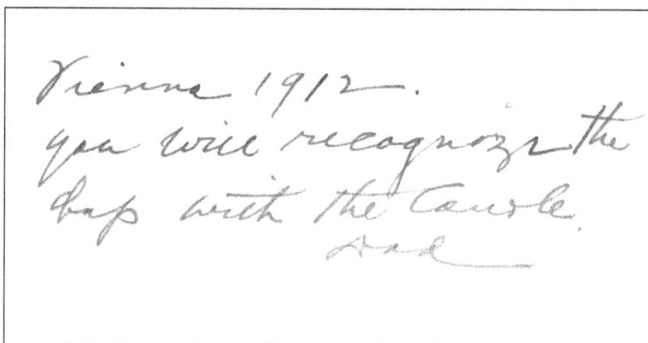

W.T.D. with fellow students at the University of Vienna, 1912, and his note on the reverse of the photo: "Vienna 1912. You will recognize the chap with the candle. Dad"

During 1911 while Assistant, Office of Attending Surgeon, he was an assistant instructor in ophthalmology and optometry at the Army Medical School.

1909–1912
At some point during this period Captain Davis did postgraduate work at the Royal Ophthalmic Hospital in London.

MAY 16, 1912
Requests assignment to Vienna, Austria, to pursue study of eye diseases in the field of ophthalmology (states that he has been on duty at Army Medical School in D.C. "for the past two years").

MAY 24, 1912
Ordered to Vienna for postgraduate school at University of Vienna, sponsored by U.S. Army.

Renée traveled to Vienna, to marry Capt. Davis. Since Vienna was predominantly Catholic they had a difficult time finding a Protestant church. Due to his status as U.S. Military officer in uniform, Capt. Davis and his fiancée were invited to a great reception at the palace of Emperor Franz Joseph I, the longest-reigning emperor of Austria, reigning for 68 years, 1848–1916. Renée was a beautiful young lady with striking auburn hair. They were wonderful dancers and danced the waltz beautifully. The Emperor noticed the dashing young couple and had his aides call them to the throne. Emperor Joseph complimented them and then asked, "Is there something I can do for you?" William said, "There surely is. We have been trying for days to find a Protestant church in Vienna to marry us. We can't find one, they are all Catholic." The Emperor responded, "I will take care of that. It shall be done." They were notified the next day where they could go to get married. William and Renée were married at one of the few Protestant churches a few days later.

SEPTEMBER 28, 1912
William Thornwall Davis and Renée HasBrouck Tolson married in Vienna, Austria. William was 35, Renée 25. The priest, knowing little English, tried to give as much of the service in English as he could. When he reached the point in the ceremony when he was to say "And now you can give the lady the ring," he mistakenly said, "And now you can give the lady the bing." William erupted into laughter and almost broke up the wedding. The priest was embarrassed because he didn't know what he had said.

SEPTEMBER 29, 1912
They honeymooned in Bavaria, and on their way there attended a service at Salzburg Cathedral. (Their fourth son, Sheldon, during his WWII march through Europe as an officer in the Army Rainbow Division, sent home in October 1945 a picture of this cathedral [see photo on the following page].) During their honeymoon they traveled and hiked in the Bavarian Alps. Renée was muscular and strong but had very weak feet, which pained her greatly. William did not know this at the time. She never complained. At a mountain inn there was a heavy pregnant German girl. She carried

In 1945 Sheldon took this photo of Salzburg Cathedral, Salzburg, Austria. Renée wrote on the back: "Dad and I went to services here the day after our marriage on Sept. 28, 1912."

their trunk on her back three flights of stairs. Renée was shocked and later said "that was awful." This girl had her baby the next day. Two days later she was back carrying trunks again.

OCTOBER 12, 1912
Graduated from University of Vienna having done special work in ophthalmology.

JULY 17, 1913
Submitted his letter of resignation of his commission as Captain, Medical Corps, U.S. Army. "My reasons for this step being, (a) that my health is not good in the tropics. (b) That I may practice the profession of ophthalmology in civil life."

NOVEMBER 15, 1913
Resignation effective. He was stationed in Washington at the time. After his resignation he was supposed to turn in his canteen and strap, one to one office, and one to another. He turned them both in to one office only. Years later he received a letter with 22 endorsements on it saying please return your strap. He wrote to the general, "You and your strap can go straight to hell."

Renée had been left some money/property in Mr. HasBrouck's will. There was enough so that when her husband left the service she was able to buy a residence at 927 17th Street, on Farragut Square in downtown Washington (in her name). (See photo on page 44.) Farragut Square is named for Admiral Farragut, whose statue stands in the middle of the square. Just one-half block from where the Army-Navy Club now stands, this building became their home and the office building where Dr. Davis would begin his ophthalmology practice. They lived upstairs, the office downstairs. Years later the family moved from Farragut Square but Dr. Davis maintained his practice there for the remainder of his life.

Office of the
Attending Surgeon, U. S. Army,
Washington, D.C. July 17, 1913.

From: Captain William T. Davis, Medical Corps,U.S.Army.

To: The Adjutant General, U.S.Army, Washington, D.C.
            (Through the Surgeon General, U.S.Army)

Subject: Resignation.

1.   I respectfully submit herewith the resignation
of my commission as Captain, Medical Corps, U.S.Army, to take
effect upon the expiration of the leave of absence granted
me in S.O.#146,W.D.,June 24,1913.

2.   My reasons for this step being, (a), that my health
is not good in the tropics. (b) That I may practice the profession
of ophthalmology in civil life. It is with regret that I seek
to separate myself from the military service but owing to the
reasons stated I feel that I can be of more service to my country
in civil life.

91013-6   1st Ind.   M.CMG/H.

War Department, S. G. O., July 19, 1913., - To The Adjutant General of the
Army, approval recommended.

                                        Surgeon General, U. S. Army.

Resignation from the Medical Corps, July 17, 1913. Reproduced at the National Archives.

JUNE 10, 1914

Their first son, William J. G. Davis (Uncle Bill), born at their home on Farragut Square. Doctors came to the house in those days to help the women give birth.

927 17th Street, Washington, D.C. — photo taken in August 1955. Purchased in 1913/14 and used as a residence/office building — first floor waiting room, second floor office, top two floors family residence. Sons Bill and Roger were born here. Bill used this as his office starting 1946.

JULY 1914 TO NOVEMBER 1918. WORLD WAR I.
World War I. W.T.D. receives a professorship of ophthalmology with the rank of Major during the war in the Army Medical School.

At some point during this period Grandpa joined the Military Order of the Carabao. The history of this organization is as follows. In the closing days of the Boxer Rebellion in China (1899–1901), officers who served in that conflict formed a military organization to perpetuate their comradeship in arms, called the Order of the Dragon. In 1900 a group of officers in Manila who served in the Philippine campaign of the Spanish–American War decided to form their own society to spoof the arrogant members of the Order of the Dragon. As a joke they called themselves the Military Order of the Carabao, named after the lowly, despised, most cursed-at and best-loved animal the forces knew: the patient water buffalo, or carabao. The carabao loves to wallow in muddy shallows so they called their annual party in Washington, D.C., the "Carabao Wallow." The carabao is a beast of cow-like demeanor and docility, so long as he stays wet, thus the Carabao herd (members) would always be "well-wetted down" (with alcohol) during the Wallows. A serious element gradually surfaced to eclipse the initial joke. The Carabao Order came to epitomize the camaraderie that grows among members of the armed forces who face the dangers and privations of extensive military service far from home. The Carabao today is arguably the largest and most privileged service club of comradeship in the world. Guests to Wallows always include a multitude of top leaders of our five uniformed services. Membership in the organization was extended to descendents and other officers serving in the South Pacific theater. Grandpa took all of his sons to Wallows after they came of age. The Davis family has been attending the Wallow for over a hundred years. Grandpa maintained extensive contact with other officers, and with many enlisted men, especially those connected to the Philippine campaign.

MARCH 22, 1917
Their second son, Roger HB. Davis (my dad), born at 927 17th Street.

JUNE 1917
Appointed to Medical Reserve Corps section of the Officer Reserve Corps. and called to active duty.

1920

Professor of Ophthalmology at George Washington University. He quickly gained eminence as a competent clinician and as a gifted teacher. Renée
wrote, "In the teaching of his students he gave them more than knowledge.
He taught them love of service and integrity." His desire to reach a larger field
in education brought about the inception of the famous George Washington
University postgraduate course in ophthalmology. Organized with his characteristic military precision, it operated with amazing smoothness.

1920

The family moved farther out from downtown Washington to 3703 North
Hampton Street in Chevy Chase, Maryland. Grandpa continued to conduct his private ophthalmology practice at the Farragut Square office.

1922

Their third son, René Sheldon Davis (Uncle Sheldon), born at their North
Hampton Street home. Dad's (Roger's) room was at the opposite end of the
upstairs hall from his parents' room. Just minutes after Sheldon was born
Grandpa burst into Roger's room and yelled, "Oh the little baby just came
down from heaven."

1923

Three feet of snow fell on Washington, D.C. in 24 hours. Grandpa's Model
T Ford couldn't be driven in the snow. Worried about his wife and three
boys, he walked home in the deep snow, about five miles.

 Doctors in Washington would normally take Thursdays off and most
of them would go to the golf course. Grandma and Grandpa would go
horseback riding (Preece Riding School). They would begin at Rock Creek
park, ride out to Massachusetts Avenue and then back through Rock Creek
Park. It was mostly all countryside then, just trails, no roads. Sometimes
they would ride all the way out to East-West Highway and beyond. Roger
would ride with them sometimes on the weekends. Instructors would say,
"Roger, you have a very good seat."

Early 1920s

They bought a 25-acre country farm on the south side of Gunston Cove (an
inlet of the Potomac River) not far below Mt. Vernon, Virginia, and close

Roger and Bill, circa 1923 — Roger approximately age six, Bill nine.

Early 1920s, Roger and Bill swimming in the Potomac at Gunston Cove Farm.

to Gunston Hall, home of U.S. Founding Father George Mason. Grandpa purchased it because he had grown up on a farm as a kid. He thought that the crops and animals would pay for it but they never did. He also bought it for the enjoyment of the family. There were two houses — they occupied the main house. When the boys' school let out they headed to the farm for their summers. They learned a lot about farm living — crops and animals. Grandpa shot quail and brought them home for dinner. Dad remembered in the Fall, flocks of ducks stretching from almost horizon to horizon (no more). The farm is where Dad learned to swim, fish and sail. Their pet dog, Scottie, was a black Scottish terrier. When strawberry season came Grandma said she couldn't find many ripe ones. The next day Grandpa told her "I saw this morning why you don't, I got up early and saw Scottie out there eating ripe strawberries." Clever Scottie would get up early and eat ripe strawberries before Grandma got out of bed. At times the family would go over to Gunston Hall, visit and have dinner with the Hurtles.

Grandma received a telephone call one day that the main house had burned down. The main house had a Kohler generator in the basement which would switch on automatically when one would flip a light. There were wash basins, bathtubs, and toilets, etc. on the first floor. Grandma went to look at the house and didn't find anything but burned wood. The aforementioned things do not burn up so it was obvious that someone had stripped the house and set it on fire. Grandpa said that it must have been

Two views of the tenant house at Gunston Cove Farm. When the main house burned down, the family moved into the tenant house after repairs and additions were made.

some "poor white trash in the area who did it." They decided to add on to the tenant house and use that as their country home.

OCTOBER 29, 1925

Their fourth son, Akin Thornwall Davis (Uncle Akin), born in a hospital. The family was living at 1601 23rd Street, Washington, D.C., and continuing to spend summers at the farm. There was an eight-year difference between Roger and Akin.

Roger with catfish at Gunston Cove Farm, approximately 1927–28.

One Sunday summer afternoon, Grandpa (age 48) and Roger (age 8) were sailing on the Potomac off the banks of their country home in their small one-sail boat. There was a group of "row-dies" partying on the beach and shoot-ing at a target. Suddenly some of their shots were fired in the direction of the boat — one bullet struck the water on one side of the boat and ricocheted to land on the other side. Grandpa became furious and red in the face, lowered the sail, told Roger to lie on the boat bot-tom, and rowed directly into the group of men. He used "words that [Roger] had never heard before," "he laid 'em out and they all cowered." He was "spunky." Grandpa said, "I am an army officer, I am retired, and I still have my Colt .45 automatic, and hereafter when I go on this river I'm going to have it on this boat, and whoever shoots at me again I'm going to come right in with it and I'm going to lay 'em out." Grandpa told Roger after the incident, "Son, that was rather foolish but, son, I don't like to be shot at." Many years later Roger told his children, "They never shot at us again and we always had that .45."

They sold the farm in approximately 1927 when the kids started to get older. Roger went back 60 years later (when he was about 70 years old) and found the property. It was hard to find and the old house was just a pile of boards, grown over with brush. He "didn't want to go back again."

Grandma (Renée) "did not do much family talk about her early years" according to Dad (Roger). The HasBroucks (who had adopted her) had a summer home in Marin County, north of San Francisco (now connected via the Golden Gate Bridge. It was called Ho Ho. A picture of the entrance to Ho Ho currently hangs in my office. We have Renée's gold locket pen-dant engraved with "Ho Ho" on one side and "T" (for Tolson) on the other — inside are pictures of her husband, William. We also have pictures of the little fawn at Ho Ho who would walk in, visit and sit next to them as if

ABOVE: The entrance to Ho Ho. BELOW: Renée's locket pendant (see locket photos in color on dust jacket).

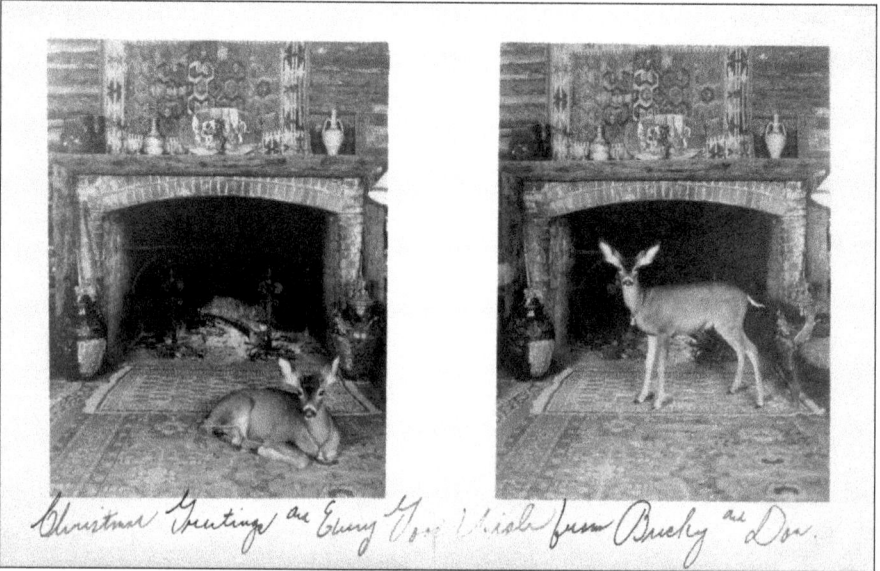

The visiting fawn at Ho Ho.

Anginette HasBrouck holding Roger at Kirk Street, San Francisco.

it were the family pet dog, then walk back into the woods. The HasBroucks had a Chinese family who worked for them at Ho Ho. Many Chinese were immigrating from China during that period. As a child, Renée had learned about the mushrooms growing there and the difference between the good and the bad. She saw the Chinese family coming back one evening with a big bucket of toadstools. She told them, "No, no, no!" but they wouldn't/ couldn't understand her. They finally shoved her away. They spent "one painful night with stomach aches and diarrhea, yelling and shrieking." They listened to Renée after that. Once, when she was quite young, one of the Chinese servants gave her a puff of opium, making her quite ill. The servant was dismissed. As a young lady in San Francisco, before meeting William, she had a suitor who "kept bringing her things and taking her out, a very sweet man." She wasn't really very interested in him. One day he said, "I want to bring you some flowers tomorrow, now you tell me what kind of flowers you want and I will get them for you." She didn't know what to think or say so she responded, "Just bring me some violets." He did so. She later learned that violets at that time of year were hard to find and cost an abominable amount. She felt very bad.

The family visited often with Anginette HasBrouck, Grandma's guard-

Bill and Roger at Kirk Street (all pictures on these two pages from San Francisco or Ho Ho).

Roger, age three.

Bill at age five.

Bill, age five and a half, and Roger, two and a half.

ian, in San Francisco and at Ho Ho. Hanging on my office wall is a picture of a cabin at Ho Ho with the inscription, written by young Akin on the back, "Aunt Nettie's and my sleeping cabin."

1928

Their home at 1601 23rd Street, NW, was located next door to the Romanian Embassy. When the Embassy offered them a price they could not refuse, they accepted and purchased a new residence in Washington at 3601 Lowell St., NW ($28,000).

Around this time, Dr. Davis had an office appointment with a young man who was applying to West Point Military Academy. Any kind of physical impediment disqualified one from the service academies and he was having trouble passing the eye examination. He had been studying night and day and his eyes were very tired. To see clearly people will often squint, but squinting during an Academy eye exam would be a tipoff to eye problems. Grandpa taught him to contract his iris without squinting and he passed the exam. Grandpa had written many medical papers and delivered numerous lectures about the condition of squinting and crossed eyes.

1932

See the Davis family Christmas greeting card from (approximately) this year, on facing page.

1933

Bill entered the University of North Carolina as a freshman.

1936

Roger entered Princeton University as a freshman. Akin lived at home for a long while after Bill and Roger left for college and Grandpa "had much association with Akin during this time."

CIRCA 1936

Dr. Davis had conceived of and been successful with a new type of surgery and treatment to fix a particular type of eye condition that caused seriously reduced vision or blindness in many thousands of children across the country. He was invited to the White House to meet with President Roosevelt. At their meeting the President commended him on his success and

The Season's Greetings
from
The Davis Family

Family Christmas card from around 1932.

June 24 to July 3, 1936: Renée, Roger and Akin travel to Europe. This photo taken in Boulogne, France, July 3, 1936.

remarked, "Wouldn't it be nice if we could do this for all of the children in this country?" The President was suggesting that maybe the government should pay for this operation and treatment for all children. Dr. Davis said yes, that would be nice, but the cost of the operation and cure was so astronomical, it would make the initiative impractical. The President told him to think about it and thanked him for his counsel. Even though Grandpa had developed this cure to help children, it annoyed him that the President would consider having the country spend so much money on another program (he did not agree with Roosevelt's big spending and big government policies). A week or two later a new patient made an appointment with Dr. Davis. Dr. Davis found nothing wrong with this patient's eyes but curiously during the appointment the man kept asking him about the aforementioned new eye cure and how wonderful it would be for all the children affected if the government would provide the cure. When Grandpa realized that this was an aide of the President's who had made an eye appointment under false pretenses, he became infuriated, took the man by the scruff of his neck and seat of his pants, ushered him down the stairs, out through the front office where other patients were waiting, and threw him into the street. Later he told Roger it had been foolish of him to do that. Uncle Akin can still remember sitting at meals hearing his Dad rant about President

Roosevelt, "chief of the swine," as he banged his fist on the dining room table.

JUNE 24–JULY 3, 1936
Renée, Roger and Akin travel to Europe. Voyaged on the ocean liner *SS Volendam*.*

SUMMER OF 1937
Family trip to Europe. Voyaged on the *Queen Mary* (photo on following page). In Switzerland Akin got sick, so Grandpa, Bill, Roger, and Sheldon visited Germany while Grandma stayed with Akin in Switzerland. Upon returning from Germany, Grandpa said, "There's going to be war, I can feel it." The war started two years later. In 2016, while visiting with Uncle Akin for a couple of days, I found a Riker mount display case of butterflies. Uncle Akin told me those were the butterflies he had collected in Switzerland in 1937 while his father and three brothers traveled to Germany.

Roger on the SS Volendam *just before the farewell banquet and ball.*

They spent many summers vacationing along the shores of Lake Kanasatka in New Hampshire at Camp Vonhurst (outside the village of Center Harbor). Vonhurst, a cottage-type camp for adults and families with around 3,800 feet of private waterfront and sixty acres of forested land, provided

---

*Four years later the *SS Volendam* was attacked by a German submarine several hundred miles off the coast of Northern Ireland. Two torpedoes hit her bow. The captain gave the order to abandon ship, and despite rough seas all 18 lifeboats got away safely. There was only one casualty. Later when she was repaired the second torpedo was found unexploded and embedded in her bow.

Summer of 1937: Renée, Bill, Roger and Akin travel to Europe on the Queen Mary. *W.T.D. joined them a week later, traveling by plane.*

swimming, fishing, hiking and a variety of other activities — ping pong, pool, badminton, deck tennis, volleyball, horseshoes, archery. Guests could stay in one of the fifteen private cottages along the lakeshore. The camp was owned and operated by Frederick H. and Lucille Von der Sump. Mr. Von (as the family knew him) was a retired minister and a carpenter — a very gentle man. He and Grandpa became good friends.

Well groomed, able, shrewd, civic minded, Grandpa served in numerous local organizations: Rotary Club, Chevy Chase Club, Military Order of the Carabao, Society of the Cincinnati of Virginia. He contributed numerous important medical papers and served in positions of influence. He was Senior Surgeon at the Episcopal Eye and Ear Hospital. Chief of service in ophthalmology at the George Washington University Hospital and consultant to other hospitals. Taught postgraduate course at George Washington University. Lectured at universities across the country. A Director of the Washington Loan and Trust Company and the Washington Society for the Prevention of Blindness. President of Washington Ophthalmology

At Camp Vonhurst, Center Harbor, New Hampshire, late 1930s or early 1940s. Back (FROM LEFT): Sheldon, W.T.D., Akin, Bill. Front (FROM LEFT): Helen, Renée.

W.T.D. and Renée at Camp Vonhurst.

Society. First vice president of the American Academy of Ophthalmology and Otolaryngology. Chairman of the executive committee of the council of the Southern Medical Association. Appointed ophthalmological consultant to the Surgeon General of the War Department in 1943. One of the eminent eye specialists in the country, he was honored by membership in a host of national and foreign military and professional organizations and in 1940 was decorated with the Order of Carlos J. Finlay. 1941 recipient of Columbian University Alumni Achievement Award. Convinced of their importance, he was a regular attendant at medical meetings in all parts of the country.

He vigorously maintained his ophthalmology practice but continued to publish papers on various eye conditions and diseases, write articles, lecture, and teach. His last lectures and publications of which we have copies are as follows: April 20–22, 1944, lecture to the University of Michigan postgraduate course on "Pseudo-Paretic Hyperphoria," and May 23, 1944, publication on "Conservation of Vision."

Following are transcriptions of various personal letters written by Dr. Davis:

MAY 1935
Letters between Grandpa and Dr. Thomas W. Sidwell, principal of Sidwell Friends School in Washington, D.C., where son Roger was a senior:

May 4, 1935
My dear Dr. Sidwell,

At dinner last night Roger spoke to me about a letter which was placed before the Senior class in which a suggestion or a request (I did not gather which) was made that all members of the class sign this letter. It was directed to the President of the United States.

My sons have been instructed by me not to sign any documents without consulting me until they are sufficiently mature to know what they are doing. This is an understanding between us. I wonder if you would be kind enough to let me have a copy of this letter or petition, so I can advise Roger.

Very sincerely,
William T. Davis

May 6, 1935

My dear Dr. Davis,

In reply to your letter of May 4, I am enclosing a copy of the paper I read to our High School pupils. It was intended to be informative of the thought in the minds of other young people and to get the reaction of ours. I did not recommend or urge them to do anything. I simply afforded them an opportunity to show by hands their approval or disapproval. Some approved, some disapproved, and some wanted more time to think about it.

Your instruction to your son in regard to signing papers is very good and meets with my approval.

After reading the paper I would be glad for any comments you have to make on it.

I like our young people to know something of present trends and to be able to express their views. As there was a difference of opinion in regard to this paper would you favor having an expression for or against from some of the pupils.

Sincerely yours,
Thos. W. Sidwell
Principal

The paper read to the senior class by Dr. Sidwell:

To the President from students and Young People of the United States

Mr. President,

We, the young people of America, call upon you to take the lead in reducing armaments in these days of international crisis, and to blaze the path toward a new international amity.

Rumors of impending wars go through the world and everywhere there is fear that another futile combat of nations, more horrible than ever before and perhaps imperiling the existence of the human race, may come at any time.

We believe that this uneasiness and the dangers which accompany it have their foundation chiefly in the race of nations in armaments.

Our country, like other countries, is in this contest. It is apparent that no matter how many battleships, guns or shells we add, other nations will make similar increases in their armaments, thus cancelling any gains we may have made in the possession of the implements of death and destruction and giving us no more security than we had before the race started.

If war comes, it is our generation that must bear the brunt of the suffering, not only in war itself, but in the economic chaos that will surely follow.

We challenge the right of the generation now guiding the affairs of the world to inflict such injury upon us. We call on you to act now to restore international good will and to diminish the fear and distrust which besets the world by having America reverse its course and take the lead in actually reducing armaments.

July 9th, 1935
My dear Dr. Sidwell,

I must ask you to pardon me for not answering your kind letter of May 6th before this. Matters have been pressing heavily and this is my first opportunity.

I appreciate your sending me a copy of the paper you read to the High School pupils. I think this was perfectly right but I feel it is incumbent upon me to say that I am not in sympathy with this attitude. The world is quite mad and destruction threatens many peoples and governments. To place our beloved country in a position of helplessness cannot but invite the same destruction that has come to China and will overcome Ethiopia; therefore the only way to obtain peace is to fight for it.

Being a veteran of two wars and having seen the horrors of both, no one could abhor it more than I, particularly when I have four sons who could be called upon to give their lives in this terrible way. However, I feel it is the only way to keep our country safe and that country whose sons will not give their blood to defend, is irretrievably and utterly lost. As one of our greatest Presidents said, 'Be properly prepared.'

This is the attitude I think we should all take and not to place ourselves in a position of helplessness so that the mail fist can crush us ere we can get ready to defend ourselves.

Hope you had a pleasant trip to Mexico. It is a charming and delightful place, isn't it? I wish that I could have been with you.

With my cordial and affectionate best wishes for a pleasant summer, believe me.

Most Sincerely,
William T. Davis

MARCH 23, 1938 – LETTER FROM GRANDPA (61) TO HIS SON ROGER ON HIS 21ST BIRTHDAY (ROGER WAS A SENIOR AT PRINCETON):
Dear son of mine,

My love and congratulations on your becoming of age. You now take on the freedom and responsibilities of life & may they come to you full of promise, hope and happiness.

If you go on as you have been going many good things will come to you. Keep sane, sober and steady. Beware of wine, women and dissipation. They lead to early decay & death — or worse. I know of no short cut to success; if there are such they would not appeal to me for success so obtained is likely to turn out a curse.

God bless you my son. You will ever have my fondest & deepest affection.

Dad

The check is your birthday present and is not part of your allowance.

Roger majored in economics at Princeton. He elected to center his graduate thesis around a topic in which he had great interest, aviation. Roger graduated May of 1939 and in the loom of war he volunteered to enter the Army reserves (inactive duty), aspiring to eventually join the Army Air Corps. On June 1, 1939, he was appointed Second Lieutenant of Field Artillery, U.S. Army Reserves. He was a civilian but could be called to active duty at any time. During Roger's senior year at Princeton Grandpa had written numerous letters to his friends in the military introducing his son and requesting their counsel concerning Roger's interest in aviation and the opportunities available. Grandpa was instrumental in helping Roger gain employment with Douglas Aircraft in Santa Monica, California.

Fortuitously, I, Robert Davis, have recently discovered a treasure trove of hundreds of letters that passed between them during the ensuing five-year period from mid-1939 to mid-1944, thus giving us the previously unimaginable opportunity to get to know this extraordinary man, William Thornwall Davis. After Roger graduated from college and left home he remained in close contact with his family, always sharing his life, his thinking, and asking for counsel. The close and confiding relationship Roger had with his father was truly remarkable. Their mutual trust along with their exceptional eloquence and articulation, made for uninhibited and clear communication. In a spirit of love and compassion, these letters give us insight and inspiration on many levels and subjects. They reveal Grandpa's deep understanding of life and his passion to pass it on to his children. This is Grandpa during his final years and Roger during his initial years — Grandpa as "the shades of evening are falling" in his life and Roger "upon the early mornings" of his life. This is a journal of what transpired between a loving father and a loving son during one of the most momentous and uncertain periods in our nation's history. This is a journal of a devoted father who was as passionate about protecting his sons as he was about best preparing them for their highest and best use by their country. These letters give us history of family, and of country. This is an opportunity to experience the wisdom, the intelligence, and the deep and unconditional love of a man for his family, his country, and, later, for the only grandchild he ever had the opportunity to know.

Grandma wrote from time to time but it was primarily Grandpa who so often wrote, counseled, and suggested to Roger. Included in many of his letters were letters and notes from Bill, Sheldon, and/or Akin (all closer to home). Phone calls were difficult and infrequent, usually only made when the entire family was together and after prior arrangement. Telegrams were for immediate communications. At the commencement of these letters Grandpa was 62 years old, Grandma 52, and Roger 22. Bill (25) was attending University of Maryland medical school and living in Baltimore with his wife, Helen (married May 1939). Sheldon (17) was at Riverside Military Academy in Gainsville, Georgia. Akin (14) living at home and attending St. Albans Prep School as a day student.

Grandpa was constantly putting Roger in touch with numerous military and family friends in the Santa Monica area who gave Roger personal support, counsel and friendship during this period. Many of Grandpa's letters included newspaper clippings about a variety of subjects: Princeton, the war, aviation, medicine, politics, environment, local events, Grandpa's events, etc. I have listed references and excerpts (some letters in their entirety) from these letters in sequence. Due to the number of letters, there are many to which I make no reference. This partial transcription does not do full justice to their communications but hopefully enough to give us a good understanding of who they were and what transpired during this period. To repeat, this collection of letters is the closest thing we have to knowing and having a relationship with this great man, William Thornwall Davis. I, Robert Davis, am 70 years old when I find, read and transcribe in part these letters. I will be eternally grateful that I have at last truly gotten to know my grandfather. Of his four sons, only Uncle Akin is alive now. Dad (Roger) died at the age of 87, eleven years ago in 2004. Oh how I wish I could have read these letters 40 years ago, I would be a better man today. Those of you who are younger have the advantage of reading them now. I would highly suggest reading carefully and alertly. I can only speak for myself here, but it is my impassioned hope that they too will inspire you to be better people, better Americans, and better mothers and fathers.

I begin with the first letter between them after Roger left home for Santa Monica. Please understand that the transcription of these letters has been a deeply emotional process for me. After much deliberation I have concluded that in deference to Grandpa and my dad, and to the reader, I must refrain from my passion to highlight important passages and interject my personal comments. Any underlining or emphasis in these transcripts is from the original letters. I make notes only where I deem appropriate for clarification and comment, and these are shown in italics, so that you can readily distinguish them from the transcripts. Hence, I leave to you your own personal thoughts, conclusions and private emotions.

July 5, 1939. Letter from Roger to Grandpa. Roger living at 304 Idaho Avenue, Santa Monica, California. In its entirety:
Dear Mom and Dad,
I have been here for four days now and it seems like a mighty long time. (Please excuse this darn type-writer; something seems to have happened to it since I last used it in Princeton. I guess it didn't weather the trip as well as I did) I arrived in Los Angeles last Sunday morning, and I can truly say that I felt a little lost. However, the first person I ran into was a boy from Princeton who was in my class. The advantages of going to a big university are already beginning to show. The boy himself was not a native of this section of the country but his grandfather was there to meet him so I was able to obtain all the information that I needed about getting to Santa Monica, etc.

I took a street car out Sunday morning and arrived in about an hour. I got a room at a small hotel for the day and started to inquire about room and board and a used car. I spent the whole day roaming from one end of Santa Monica to the other trying to find what I wanted in the way of an automobile but without much luck. It seems that there just isn't a market for heavy used cars. The few I did find had not been reconditioned in any way and had no guarantee, so I was a little hesitant about buying one of them. Also, most of the used cars for sale were handled by used car dealers who were not in any other business. Very few were sold by reputable sales people and garages. After much deliberation I got a 1934 Ford business coup which had been completely (reconditioned) by the Ford people here and was guaranteed by them. I have driven it about 250 miles already and it seems to run like a bird. To all appearances it is in very good condition. All I hope is that appearances are not deceiving.

This morning I went out to the Douglas Plant *(in El Segundo)* which is about three miles inland from here (I am located only about three blocks from the shore). I spent about four hours going from one desk to another giving my life's history at each one. About lunch time I went to Los Angeles to get my Social Security number and then reported back to the plant. I then had a long talk with several of the men about what type of work I could best do as I had no training in engineering. It is a good thing I decided to take Accounting and Corporation Finance last year because as far as I can gather now I am starting work tomorrow morning at 7:30 in the accounting division of the Engineering Department. Wish me luck.

It is getting rather late and I'm afraid the type-writer is keeping the rest of the people awake so I'll sign off. I will write very soon again and tell you about the place I am staying and more about the job.

Your loving son, Rog

July 8, 1939. Grandpa to Roger (5 pages). This letter written two days before Roger started his new job in Santa Monica. In its entirety:

Dear Rog,

So nice to have your letter dear son and to know you are located, have your car and your job.

I have sent it on to mother by via air mail. It reached me the early afternoon the following day. Some service. Letter from Bill & Helen. Wonderful time; ideal boat, weather, moon, sea, people, et cetera et cetera.. Very happy letters and appreciative. I am sure we will enjoy their happiness with them will we not? Mother left on Wednesday the fifth for Nantucket. Wire from her saying they had arrived safely after a very pleasant trip. Today is 105 degrees and I am glad you are in the land where excessive heat isn't so bad.

I hope you got Mr. Spillsbury's letter. I suggest you call upon him in due season. They are English & Canadian & somewhat formal. Punctiliousness in you will be appreciated.

The car you purchased sounds good. Dear son may I caution you about keeping yourself fit mentally, physically, and morally. It pays <u>handsome</u> dividends mentally, physically & morally, <u>and</u> financially. The fit succeed, the unfit rarely and then not continually. Get sufficient rest and exercise so you can be on the job <u>alert</u>. You <u>cannot</u> if you are fatigued & you will be fatigued if you do not have rest and exercise. Please don't think Dad is preaching. Only my love and pride in you prompts me to say this.

There are no sheltering safeguards now — only your habits and character and conscience. May our dear Lord guide you.

All goes well at home. The roses are lovely & home is sweet & quiet & relatively cool after the heat of the downtown with its clutter & bang. You experienced the value of the prestige of a high class university very promptly. But keep it quiet & don't lean on it.

Fondest love dear son and all good luck in your work. We shall be happy to hear about it. We will file your letters as per agreement; they will make a happy reading later on and no mean record. I leave on July 22nd for Rochester N.Y. & from there to Nantucket. After this date write us there.

Cheerio, Dad

JULY 9, 1939. ROGER TO GRANDPA. EXCERPTS:

I scouted around Sunday and Monday looking for a car and a place to room, finding both ... the room is turning out to be much better than expected. The landlady, Mrs. Howard, is quite a character and has placed herself as a guardian mother over me. She is so interested in what I am doing.

The other day she had a confidential talk with me saying that there were two kinds of crowds to run around with, the right and the wrong. She hoped that I would choose the right crowd and if I wanted to know some nice people she would be only too glad to introduce me. So you see I have even found personal interest out here ... I have taken all of my meals out as Mrs. Howard doesn't serve them here ... Dinner can be had from 25 cents to 75 cents at many places around Santa Monica. The 25 cent one is a little cheap if the appetite is ravenous, but the 75 cent one is too much and too good to eat at one sitting no matter how hungry one is. Consequently my dinner usually costs me around 40 cents.

Now to what happened to me the first days of my working life last week

... no one could decide exactly what kind of work I might do as I was only going to be with the factory temporarily anyway ... The job I was finally assigned was that of timekeeper in the shops. This consists of filling out a card every time a workman changes from one job to another and noting the time. In this way it is possible to tell just where every part of an airplane is and how much time is being spent in its fabrication. Also, by this constant check on the men there is little chance for them to waste any time or to do work for their personal needs.. Being a new man all the workmen try to put something over on me ...

Finances are still OK but a little low as I forgot that any check I deposited (from you) would be no good until it cleared through Washington and returned here. Paying for the car took all the cash I had except for enough to buy food for a week.. The present job pays about $80 per month..

I have tried to locate the Boones at Long Beach, I think that is where you said they lived, but could not do so. Could you send me their address? Also I called on Mr. and Mrs. Spillsbury this afternoon but did not find them at home ...

... I am on my feet walking all day, so if you think I am going to get my exercise walking during the weekends somebody is mistaken. I am going to have to figure something else out ...

JULY 15, 1939. GRANDPA TO ROGER (6 PAGES). EXCERPTS:
My thoughts have been constantly with you these days 'out in the wide wide world.' That you will comport yourself in sense & safety & refrain from too much liberty is my assurance and satisfaction. I am thankful for your sense and stability which will stand you in good stead for there will be many and severe temptations awaiting you. That you will have the stamina and good sense to recognize them I have not the slightest doubt. As you see from Mother's letter we have the same house at Nantucket — Come if you find things going too bad. Home, God bless it, is here waiting for you with love and affection. 'Here' means where we are son, for your place is ever with us when you want it.

I am pushed hard myself just now, heavy surgery, heavy office & many complications. Thank God I can still take it on the chin.

Bill & Helen will be here tomorrow, Sunday & they have a lot to do. I am leaving the 23rd for Rochester N.Y. where I will be at the University Club the 24th, Schenectady on the 25th to interview the G.E. about my

'Electric Eye,' Boston the 26th at the Mass. General Hospital to see about an assistant and from there to Sconset (Nantucket) ...

Just back from a glorious horseback ride. Now if you were here what a grand bull session we could have. I wish I were with you today in person as I am in spirit.

Hope you will find some fishing..

Just wrote the Boones that you are there.. I know they will be glad to see you.. he will be stationed at the Naval Dispensary at Long Beach.. write your local address on your cards, this is proper & regulations in the Navy. Your letter was grand & will be filed in the archives. We enjoy them so much & eagerly await them ...

Letter from brother Bill enclosed. Grandpa shared most of Roger's letters with Bill, Sheldon, and Akin. Bill wrote, "Rog boy, we sure have enjoyed your letters — they really are masterpieces."

JULY 15, 1939. ROGER TO GRANDPA (AND ALWAYS TO FAMILY). EXCERPT:

... And speaking about Princeton; it surely seems far away at the moment. Also, what I learned there doesn't seem to be giving me much assistance. A clear head and the ability to handle the men correctly without antagonizing them seem to be the essentials necessary for success in my work." *Roger expresses that he is working in California for Douglas Aircraft* "to gain experience and to find out whether I really wanted to go into the engineering end of aviation."

AUGUST 21, 1939. ROGER TO GRANDPA. EXCERPTS:

(Roger had learned to fly in Washington before he left for California. He has now started to fly for pleasure at the Santa Monica Airport. He also continues to connect with Grandpa's referred friends.)

... I spent a very pleasant weekend with the Boones ...

My flying is coming along very well. The ship that I use is almost new and is very sporty looking. In fact the other day, it was being cleaned so that a studio could use it in one of their movies. Dad, it is the same kind of ship that we were looking at just before I left Washington, low wing, dark color and very substantial looking.

I just heard the rumor that Douglas is making a new flying bomb for the Navy. The craft consists of a very flimsy body which encases a tremendous torpedo. The plane is supposed to climb to a height where antiaircraft guns cannot reach it and then dive straight down on the battle ship. Just before reaching it the bomb or torpedo is released and the now unbalanced plane can try to fly away. It has no boat for landing in the water and only a small landing gear for land. The fuel capacity is very small too, so that the flight of one of these planes will practically be a suicide affair. What won't they think of next ...

AUGUST 25, 1939 – ROGER TO GRANDPA. EXCERPT:
Roger has mutually agreed with his boss that he will leave his job at the end of August for world travel.

... I think that date will give me plenty of time to do my traveling, if there is much of it. It is evident that the situation in Europe is growing worse every day and it is only a question of time before the war comes. This time England refuses to back down and Germany increases her demands. Of course this has happened before but it cannot keep happening without having some consequences ... I would not give anything for the few months I am spending out here. I am finding out so much about myself and other people too.

AUGUST 31, 1939 – ROGER TO GRANDPA. EXCERPTS:
I thought for a few days that the situation in Europe was growing a little better but the paper tonight seems to give an indication that it is getting no better fast. If things do break over there I don't imagine there will be much traveling for me, as you say, Dad. In that case I have no choice of continuing my job or going to engineering school. At this moment I really don't know which I would do. I think I will pay Mr. Spillsbury a call to see what he thinks of the situation. What I want to find out most of all is whether I should have some engineering to enter the <u>airlines</u>, because if I did remain with my job it would be with the intention of changing to another position with one of the airlines at a later date. The only thing to do now, though, is to just sit and wait ... ¶ The work at the plant is still progressing as usual. I learn a little more each day and become more proficient in making my subtractions on the time cards. I figured out today that I make about 4,000 computations every two weeks, and during the last two weeks I made about 10 mistakes. That isn't so bad but it still can be improved upon ... ¶ The only reason that I had the time to make the foolish discovery that I just mentioned above is that the work at Douglas is slowing down a great deal. It can be sensed all over the plant. The men get into more trouble, do less

work when they do work and everybody is a little sleepy. Douglas has plenty of work to do, but the head man of that show was a little overconfident of a certain bomber that the Army was about to buy. The rush at the plant during the last month was to clear the way for the production of the new planes. Well, in the last government contract Douglas was not included at all so the routing of all the ships now in production has to be changed and a few men laid off because the anticipated rush never came, I am thankful timekeepers are still needed anyway. ¶ I just had a very pleasant interlude. Mrs. Howard came to the door with a piece of ice-cold watermelon for me. I was feeling thirsty so it really hit the spot. Now when I finish this letter I can take a short walk to the mail box and then go to bed at 9:30. And it is usually that hour when I retire. If it is any later I feel it the next day ...

SEPTEMBER 1, 1939 – Germany invades Poland, with subsequent declarations of war on Germany by France and the United Kingdom. History marked this as the beginning of World War II.

SEPTEMBER 6, 1939 – ROGER TO GRANDPA. EXCERPT:
Roger has been doing much thinking about his situation. The advice he has received:
    ... with the world in such a condition as it will soon be because of the war it will be the war industries and the war industries only where there will be much chance for advancement ... the experience and training at Douglas would be invaluable.. the best plan is (for me) to continue at Douglas for the present.

SEPTEMBER 13, 1939. ROGER TO GRANDPA. EXCERPTS:
With the situation in Europe unstable and not conducive for travel, Roger's plans have changed, and he will permanently be at Douglas.
    It seems very difficult to realize that my plans have changed and that I am remaining here in California for an indefinite length of time. At the moment home seems to be far away, and I can truthfully say that I felt very blue and almost cried when I fully realized that I would not be returning to Washington for a long time. But I do think it is for the best ... ¶ I have been watching my weight since I arrived here because it is a fairly good index of my health. While it has not gone up it has not gone down, so I guess I am holding my own.

SEPTEMBER 17, 1939 – GRANDPA TO ROGER (7 PAGES). EXCERPTS:

... Mother will leave on Tuesday the 26th & be with you on Friday 29th. Her dear heart is pining to see you.. ¶ *(concerning Roger's change of plans to leave on his travel to Europe)* The night letter we sent you on Friday & which reached you so late because of the stupidity of the Santa Monica office was merely to have you feel that you have a free choice in this matter & are not bound in any way to do what you feel we want you to do dear son. We want you to do what you desire and think best. We are behind you a hundred percent on whatever that may be. It is probably better for you to adhere to the plan you now have. We too feel lumps in our throats when we know your beautiful plans had gone awry but that is only a temporary postponement & you will be home again & have your trip just the same.. I am glad you were not in Europe; that would have been a bit messy. ¶ Don't you think it may perhaps be best for you to wait until Mother comes before finally deciding on living quarters ... (she) would be a great help to you. We want you to be comfortably cared for son. Whatever you decide upon make it decent & as homelike as possible. If you need more income it will be at your disposal. ¶ We are only 17 hours apart son so that isn't far. California used to be far away but no more. Whenever you can get time to come home we will be so happy to have you take the plane. We will gladly pay the fare. It will always be understood son that we will do that. ¶ The fellow you have chummed up with sounds good. We are so pleased that you would pick a simple nice chap; it reminds me of how Uncle George and I became friends which friendship has lasted a lifetime. He too was and is a simple nice fellow. ¶ We are so grateful that you are caring for your health. Wise wise man you are to do this. It gives us much comfort that you show such good sense and judgement in your affairs. ¶ Son, $80 a month is not a living wage for people like us but one has to have some help when one is getting started and it gives us so much pleasure to do this. You know my dear boy that my deepest satisfaction is to do for those I love. Selfish pleasures have no attraction for me. ¶ We are carefully filing your letters and a few years from now they will be so interesting and instructive for you. ¶ The old Packard is being traded in together with the old jalopy. We get a new car — Packard — for $1,055. The 37 model we now have was a defective can. It has been in the shop about once a week since we had it. ¶ An officer of the F.A. regular army told me he would rather have a Princeton ROTC man than a West Pointer. In six months he said, he could make an accomplished artillery officer of him. ¶ You read Lindbergh's radio address

I am sure. *(Col. Charles A. Lindbergh gave an address supporting American nonintervention in World War II.)* That is exactly where I stand and Mother too. She and I had discussed it and said just what he did in almost identical words. I trust and hope that is what we will do. I am absolutely opposed to entangling with Europe. The army naturally doesn't feel that way about it but the army knows but little outside the technical art of war. I am of the opinion that Congress will change the present neutrality law. Whether they do or not the airplane manufacture's will have all they can do as I am sure we will have a powerful air armada. Much in excess of that we have now. ¶ Would you care for the N.Y. Times? ... If you do I will be glad to send it to you ... ¶ Fondest love my dear son. Our love and thoughts are always with you. May the dear Lord watch over & keep you always.

Devotedly, Dad

Grandpa mailed Roger monthly checks (approximately $25) to help him with his finances. Grandpa kept a notebook of all of Roger's letters from July 9, 1939 to October 20, 1942. We have the notebook, from which I have here transcribed his letters in part.

September 18, 1939 – Roger to Grandpa. Excerpts:
.. I believe that as long as I am here I had better stay. Mr. Spillsbury's advice still seems to be holding good. From the looks of the new developments in Europe it seems that war is getting even closer to us. Russia's going into Poland with possibility that Turkey will desert England and France to remain with Russia makes it very dangerous for the democracies. Quite a few of the regular reserve have been called from the plant to do some extra training, so whether we go to it or not I think that my present position is the best until conditions become a little more settled ... ¶ ... I reported to Douglas that I would not be leaving ... would now be getting a pay raise of $1 per week ... ¶ My flying is coming along very well. In about a month I hope to go up for my private pilot's certificate ...

October 1939
Grandma visits Roger for two weeks.

October 8, 1939 – Roger to Grandpa. Excerpts:
(New apartment: 833 Ocean Avenue, Santa Monica, California.)

Mom has been here about a week now and it seems like she has just arrived. It surely is wonderful having her out here for a visit. The only sad part is that the whole family cannot be here. Mom has been marvelous to Herb and me. She takes us out to dinner every night to a new place and really gives us a good feed. One evening she cooked us a bully steak dinner here at the apartment. And to top it all she has been getting up every morning to cook us breakfast. I told her not to do it but she said that she enjoyed getting up at that hour because the weather was so beautiful at that time of day. Also she said that she is going to bed at an early hour like Herb and me and so did not need to sleep any later. ¶ We are really very comfortable here in our new apartment ...

NOVEMBER 17, 1939. ROGER TO GRANDPA.

Roger working out the expenses for purchasing a plane — looking at a few different planes. (Dad told me that Grandpa had given him a college monthly allowance and told him "what he didn't spend was yours," and added that he eventually paid for his plane with the money that he had saved during college.) Excerpts from letter: ... Mom, it was wonderful having you out here for the visit. You were so nice to Herb and me. I am afraid that you spoiled us though with all that you did. We are finding it difficult to return to the old way of living. When we wake up in the morning we seem to forget that it is some one's turn to cook the breakfast and it almost goes uncooked. ¶ Dad, you asked me what I thought of the act just passed by Congress.* I am somewhat like you in that I do not really know what to make of the whole situation. It does seem though that it provides a better bulwark against our entering the war than the previous embargo act. As I said in my last letter it appears to be the trading, not the manufacture and selling that causes the tense situations. If the United States does not have anything to do with the actual trading, i.e. the transportation of commodities, I agree with the administration that there is less cause for trouble.

---

*Spurred by a growth of isolationism and noninterventionist sentiment after WW1, a series of Neutrality Acts were passed by Congress from 1935 to 1937 to ensure that the U.S. would not again become entangled in foreign conflicts. In September 1939, after Great Britain and France declared war on Germany, President Roosevelt came before Congress and lamented that the Neutrality Acts could give aid to an aggressor nation. He prevailed, and on November 4 the Neutrality Act of 1939 was passed, allowing for arms trade with belligerent nations (Great Britain and France) on a cash-and-carry basis, in effect ending the arms embargo.

The attitude that Mr. Hoover took seemed to me to be more sentimental and humane than practical and expedient. He wanted to prevent the shipment of all offensive weapons of war. This type of embargo might lessen the slaughter in Europe to a small degree but I believe defensive weapons would be just as bad as any other type of war material as far as causing the belligerents to object to our transporting goods to their respective enemies. All this seems to be the stand that I take but I know that it is not very clear for the simple reason that it is not clear in my own mind ...

NOVEMBER 24, 1939. GRANDPA TO ROGER (10-PAGE LETTER). EXCERPTS:
... Bill & Helen spent Thanksgiving with us.. Bill was working almost all the time he was here on the intricacies of the nervous system. It is so much more complicated than it was in my student days that I have to learn much of it over again. Mostly the nomenclature is new; the basic facts largely unaltered ... ¶ *Concerning Roger's interest in buying a plane:* ...The maintenance of a ship must be considerable. The upkeep of a motor car is considerable, a ship must be more. I want you to have a ship but I am wondering if now is the time. This I leave to your good judgement. Whatever you decide to do <u>I am back of you</u>. I want to help in the purchase price and the maintenance to the limit of my ability. Keep me advised ... The explanation in your letter is quite dear son. It is a matter which you must decide for yourself. I am not sufficiently informed to advise you. I don't want you to get in a place where financial pressure is too great for safety or your well being in your living; Food, relaxation, play which one <u>must</u> have. If one doesn't play one soon gets stale & that is very bad. Mother and I appreciate your frank letter about the matter. It is gratifying indeed dear boy that you should take us into your confidence and we appreciate it deeply ...

NOVEMBER 24, 1939. ROGER TO GRANDPA. EXCERPT:
... please do not worry about my flying. I know the value of being cautious and will not fly anything that is dangerous. The vast majority of air accidents, unlike many car accidents, are the fault of the pilot who took chances or didn't see that his plane was in good condition. It is not my ambition to be the best pilot in the world but the <u>oldest</u>.

DECEMBER 4, 1939. ROGER TO GRANDPA. EXCERPTS:
I just returned from downtown where Christmas decorations are in

full display. I never thought that sunny Santa Monica could look at all like Christmas. What impressed me most was the cool fog rolling in from the ocean. It was the first really dense fog this year and looked like snow swirling around the buildings and holiday decorations. Unless the weather becomes a little cooler I think I am going to become a bit homesick for a touch of winter ... My flying is getting better and better. I am making fewer and fewer bad landings and am feeling much more confident, but you need not have fear that I will ever feel overconfident. Too many have done that before me.

DECEMBER 12, 1939. ROGER TO GRANDPA. EXCERPTS:
.. Last Friday night I went to the Christmas dance at the Westlake School (that is where Betty Bassett goes. Mother met her.) It was a formal affair so I gaily dressed myself in my tux and had a quite gay time. The girls were from about 12 years old to eighteen or nineteen. Of course the young ones had their dance first and went home soon after the 'old' affair commenced. Shirley Temple the movie star was there as she attends the school. She was much smaller than I had anticipated and much nicer. She was really very nice and seemed quite unspoiled by all her fame and money.. ¶ My work at the plant is becoming heavier and heavier every day. I am now doing twice the work I was doing a few months ago. Of course I am much more able to do so but still the amount I have is too much ... ¶ .. aside from the interests held by any normal boy of 22 I have interest only in flying. I shall continue to spend most of my weekends at the airport ...

DECEMBER 20, 1939. GRANDPA TO ROGER (9 PAGE LETTER). EXCERPTS:
We enjoyed your last letter so much. We always enjoy them son. You just don't realize how much they mean to us. How we shall miss you at Christmas time no one can know. Sheldon arrives at 5 A.M. tomorrow & Scott, Mommie & Adie *(Akin)* are going to the station to meet him! I have a detached retina operation and cannot get there. So it goes in a surgeons life.. ¶ .. Vivian *(nanny, housekeeper, etc.)*, Della *(cook)*, and Leonard *(chauffeur)* all join in sending you messages of greeting. A heart full of love for you dear lad & may our dear Lord be with you.

As ever and always. Your devoted Dad.

CHRISTMAS DAY, 1939. GRANDPA TO ROGER (11 PAGES AND LETTERS FROM BILL, HELEN, SHELDON AND AKIN ENCLOSED). EXCERPTS:

... Dear dear boy how we did miss you. Dear Mother, who you are so much like, said nothing but her dear heart yearns for you. Oh, so deeply! Your box of presents was wonderful Rog. So beautifully done up. It touched our hearts to think of you doing it all yourself with your limited time. Rog my son you are a comfort to our hearts and our love for you is as boundless as space.. ¶ Should I fly to Pittsburgh, Cleveland, Buffalo and points west.. The Lockheeds are not so good.* Low cabins, crowded for space & very rough. Speedy but most uncomfortable. The vibration prevents reading. Here are two facts you might think upon. Ventilation — poor. If one gets sufficient fresh air it is drafty. Windows — badly spaced so that one has difficulty in seeing the terrain. Monoxide: when I flew to Memphis in November arrived with a severe headache & exhausted. I never have headaches & 6 to 8 hours on a plane should not be exhausting. Dr. X. from Baltimore was with me and he had the same symptoms. I am sure it was monoxide.

DECEMBER 27, 1939. ROGER TO GRANDPA. EXCERPT:
.. It was wonderful talking to all of you on the telephone Christmas. It just didn't seem possible that you were 3000 miles away. All of your voices sounded so familiar except Akin's. I just couldn't believe he had a man's voice. It doesn't look like there are any more little boys in the Davis family. So don't forget, Akin, you are now to act like a man in every respect. Dad, I want to thank you ever so much for the chance to talk to all. I felt a little blue at first on Christmas because I was so far from home, but the phone conversation, even though it made me feel a little worse immediately afterwards, was a great joy to me and has made me feel very happy since.

JANUARY 3, 1940. ROGER TO GRANDPA. EXCERPT:
At Douglas Roger had ambitions to advance "to the top" — he was always looking for opportunities to train and improve himself.
... I am inclined to believe that it is a trained mind plus energy and the desire to fight to the top that is the secret to success. There is nothing remarkable in that thought, <u>but</u> it also seems to me that the latter of the two, i.e. energy and the desire, is the much more important. I may be wrong because I have not much experience to draw from, but from what I have observed during the last six months it seems to be true.

---

*Lockheed was the first aviation company in the U.S. to manufacture jet-powered aircraft.

JANUARY 7, 1940. GRANDPA TO ROGER (11 PAGES). EXCERPTS:

... Akin and Nippy *(their dog)* are having a rough house all over the place which is nice because the house is so quiet since Sheldon left *(to go back to military academy)* and it makes us feel sad.. ¶ I cannot make definite plans as yet for going to the Coast. I am pretty close to my work now and there are many and heavy demands upon me. After the Post Graduate Courses are completed I shall be easy in my mind & can <u>probably</u> fit in a week about April.. ¶ God grant that you may always have the 'little' boy feeling you spoke of <u>so</u> beautifully in your letter. It touched us the bottom of our hearts.

With this letter he enclosed an article about how one had difficulty in understanding what President Roosevelt was saying in his speeches because he would distract you with his charm.

JANUARY 20, 1940. GRANDPA TO ROGER (11 PAGES). EXCERPTS:

... Sheldon's marks for the week are *(all around 90)*. The boy is making <u>effort</u>; that is what counts. Akin is quiet and steady student and stands 1,2,3 in his class. This is <u>good</u> at St. Albans. Barring accidents he will go steadily through prep. school & to Princeton. He is so much like you that I call him Rog about half the time. The pace that you set is a stimulus to him my son. Note what example means, to your brothers now, to your sons and/or daughters in the future. Which leads me to this thought my boy, when the right girl is found don't lose her. ¶ Dad & mother are behind you. Home, family and those about you that you love are the greatest values in life; this is my personal experience and after a hard & bitter youth I believe this to be so ... ¶ ..Mother & I have just talked over your tentative plans. She thinks as do I that it would probably be wise for you to hold the job unless the war clouds lifted. This of course dear son is for <u>you</u> to decide. Ours is an advisory board only. If you decide this is the wiser course we will plan to have our vacation with you in Santa Monica. Mother, Akin, Sheldon & I will drive out and spend the summer there ... ¶ ... The talk *(on the telephone)* was grand & cheered us much. We could not hear you well. Hereafter when we get a poor connection you, having made the call, ask for the operator and have her give you a good connection. Since we pay good money for it we are entitled to a good connection.. If you do not catch up with Mr. Spillsbury today do so as soon as you can and advise me. I will know then how to proceed *(in helping Roger get into a training course)*. We have many mutual friends with Mr. Douglas and I am sure can bring this about but we must be careful and not do anything that would hurt you.. ¶ Think of but don't fret about the future, Your steady habits & hard work will win just as they did in school & college.

JANUARY 23, 1940. ROGER TO GRANDPA. EXCERPT:
.. The clippings about the Potomac freezing over were very interesting. I can remember one winter when we were at the farm that the river was frozen over at that point, but to have it frozen so solid from Key Bridge to the salt water is something new ...

JANUARY 28, 1940. GRANDPA TO ROGER (10 PAGES). EXCERPTS:
Mother and Akin are seeing 'Gone With the Wind'. I stayed an hour but could endure no more. The destruction of the aristocracy that was once was too much. I have striven all my life to forget it and forgive the canaille who accomplished it. When the destruction of Atlanta came upon the screen I could remain no longer. *(Grandma wrote in a separate letter that he "couldn't stand the misery of the south so departed.")* ¶ *Addressing Roger's quandary as to whether he should change departments for training opportunities:* "I do not have to tell you dear son that all I have to give belongs to my sons. In you I live & my deepest gratification is to help you. One must proceed cautiously else harm instead of assistance may result. Hence advise me fully so I may know how to proceed" ... ¶ ..the Potomac is frozen from its source to the bay ... Sheldon is proceeding well at his military school — has changed much — steadier, studious, and earnest — a fine and splendid lad. *(Talks to Roger about helping Sheldon get a job at Douglas.)* All are well and happy *(at home)* except for the absences of our loved ones. Those things must be endured but it is hard isn't it son? The family joins me in fondest love to you dear son. We do enjoy your letters <u>so much</u>. Thank you for them.

FEBRUARY 5, 1940. GRANDPA TO ROGER (7 PAGES). EXCERPT:
Carabao dinner (Wallow) last night; Bill was with me & how we did wish for you. It was the usual thing & quite diverting ...

FEBRUARY 8, 1940. ROGER TO GRANDPA. EXCERPT:
... Last Sunday morning Dr. Boone telephoned asking me to come for

dinner in the afternoon as Suzie was having some friends from college. I accepted naturally and found that the dinner was on one of the ships. I don't know which one as the whole group of us went on a sightseeing tour of all of the ships at anchor before arriving at our ship after dark. The dinner on board was excellent, so much better than I would expect. But of course we were served in the Admiral's cabin, and I suppose that makes a difference...

FEBRUARY 8, 1940. LETTER FROM RENÉE (GRANDMA) TO ROGER WITH ADVICE ON NOURISHMENT. EXCERPT:

... it would be a good thing to buy a small roasted chicken at a good delicatessen shop and just make bread and butter sandwiches to eat along with the big pieces of chicken — it won't seem so much like a sandwich lunch. Also use lots of butter and the best milk, that which has the greatest butter fat content. ... Monday I am going to a musical at the White House ...This week has been full of social things as it was the week before last. Today I have a luncheon, a lecture and a concert — that is some afternoon.

FEBRUARY 10, 1940. GRANDPA TO ROGER (15 PAGES). EXCERPTS:

Akin ... was towards the top of his class ... a steady student. Quite a modest little chap. He has plenty of steel in his spinal column. This is a necessity and thank goodness all you boys have it. It comes in handy does it not? ¶ *Responding to Roger's letter about a recent demanding work week:* You had a tough week son and that was where your good physique and good habits and clean living come in. You could take it & keep your head clear and your reserve power on call. Something to have that reserve power isn't it. Remember to keep it. How? Sufficient daily rest; daily exercise; daily good food and a calm mind and demeanor. The last you fortunately possess as a heritage from your lovely mother. ... I admire your spirit and determination my son. Never stop wishing and working for what you desire. One may accomplish what one desires if the iron determination and will is behind it and this you have. I think it can be done for you, since you have these qualifications. I have always felt that where one had a full and complete determination to accomplish a given thing it could be accomplished. This has been my experience in life. It will be yours I am quite sure. ... ¶ But we are to see that you are brought to the notice of the proper people ... It would be well if you use your advantages. If there is a Princeton Club I suggest your joining it. Social advantages are advantages when properly used, you intuitively would. Do you read the papers daily? That is a real advantage. Also keep your brain active by some study along your line every day — even though it is only fifteen minutes. Your education permits of selective reading and I suggest you ascertain along what lines it would be most helpful & begin to build an aeronautic library <u>now</u>; reading the material as you get it. This will put you at once at an advantage ... ¶ San Francisco has a 'Corral' of the Carabaos. It may be of advantage to you later to go to their annual 'Wallow.' You are a hereditary member. Bear it in mind.

Grandpa knew people in all levels of the government and military — he was always wisely and cautiously using his contacts and influence where he could to help Roger, never overstepping propriety. He constantly shared information which could give Roger an <u>advantage</u>. Though with all of this direction, coaching, and counsel it was always up to Roger to pursue his own success.

FEBRUARY 18, 1940. GRANDPA TO ROGER (15 PAGES). EXCERPTS:
(Roger had told Grandpa that he was worried about some friends of his who had just gotten married and had little money to make a go of it.)

... remember your dear mother and I began life with <u>no</u> income in sight. The determination to succeed, faith in one's ability to do so, true respect and devotion to one another, high ideals & precepts will overcome many obstacles. That couple <u>is</u> tackling a tough future. If they remain true they can and will surmount their difficulties and develop stamina and character in doing so. Give them my love and blessing and my hope that all may prosper with them. <u>True</u> love — which is always unselfish is the guiding light of life. They who find it have more than the wealth of the Incas. Material wealth is so often a curse. Spiritual wealth never.. ¶ Nice of Capt. Boone to have you for such a nice party with the Navy. We look forward with <u>so</u> much joy to seeing them. They are true blue and loyal friends & wc have a deep affection for them. We all shall have some good times together this summer.. ¶ ..Your yearning for home dear son is shared by mother and me and Akin too. Never do we look in your room that our heart does not ache a bit for you. We are happy though in the thought that you are in a work you love, that you are contented & comfortable & safe..

FEBRUARY 22, 1940. ROGER TO GRANDPA. EXCERPT:
... Mom, don't worry about my lunches. The cold lunch Herb and I make every day is much better than we can buy at the plant. Apparently

Early 1940s. Akin with Renée on F Street in downtown Washington. This photo taken by a street photographer, who would take pictures and then ask subjects to buy.

I am thriving on it because I have gained about six pounds since my arrival here in California, and never felt better in my life. I still play basketball twice a week with the second team at Douglas Aircraft. ..

MARCH 1, 1940. ROGER TO GRANDPA. EXCERPT:
Roger has purchased a plane.

.. The plane I have is a 'Dart'. Dad, you will remember seeing one at the field in Washington, a short stubby, low-wing monoplane. It is about a year and a half old, has been flown for about 100 hours (corresponds to 10,000 miles of driving) and is in the best of shape..

APRIL 7, 1940. GRANDPA TO ROGER (8 PAGES). EXCERPTS:
The Pansies are gorgeous, the Forsythia is yellow as gold and tomorrow our Japanese Cherry will be in full bloom & in another day or so the flowering Crab *(crabapple)* will burst into fragrance and color. Would that you were here to enjoy it with us. We planted the last names last Autumn together with quite a number of pink & white dogwoods so we have a really lovely back lawn. You shall enjoy it later. We have plans for your consideration which we shall lay before you shortly. ¶ Sheldon's last

average is 87 ... the Kid is putting forth endeavor. He appreciates the effort and expense that mother made in going to Florida at an inopportune time ... Bill is working day & night <u>very</u> hard. Is making good too. Helen is supporting him like a good fellow.. Akin quiet serene goes on with his work (attending St. Albans prep school — living at home) without a comment and apparently with ease. He is a fine kid. ¶ I enclose a clipping of the course on aviation medicine. It has created quite a sensation among the services and the civilian doctors in this hemisphere. Incidentally it has enabled me to contact the chief surgeons of the most important air lines. Pan American, T.W.A., Eastern Air. They are keen men and <u>pioneers</u>. It is a new specialty in medicine and only the alert ones realize this. We had many from West Indies and all parts of the U.S. I shall send you the stenotyped notes of this course. Some of it will be not entirely understandable to you. Skip it. Much of it will be <u>valuable</u> to you. Read it. <u>It will</u> give you something those about you will not have and that is a **great** advantage. Your excellent education will enable you to understand most of the course even though it is technical medicine. That is where a good basic education is of such great value. When you read this course you will appreciate your AB Princeton 1939 ... ¶ Dear son, I do appreciate from my heart your speaking of the allowance. Permit me out of my affection for and confidence in you to continue the same allowance for yet awhile. I know you will use it carefully and well and save the surplus for the day when you will need it. 'Tis our pleasure to do this. Emergencies will arise: car, health, plane and what not. You may have immediate need before we can be reached to respond. We are so happy that you are doing so nicely — you would beloved son. But only when <u>your</u> son makes good will you realize our gratification..

APRIL 14, 1940. GRANDPA TO ROGER. (8 PAGES). EXCERPTS:

.. Cold (28 degrees) snowing.. All the beautiful cherry & tulip trees blossoms killed. The Cherry Blossom Queen too. A chilly time on the Basin last night I imagine. I hope she had her red flannel undies on. Have you any perforated paper for you to write your letters on? I am keeping your letters & they are difficult to file when on other paper.. ¶ .. I know how much joy you get out of caring for that plane *(Roger's Dart)*. It takes me back to my Barnes White Flyer bicycle and later our first Ford car. Enjoy it old fellow and I am with you in spirit. You have earned it yourself by your self denial and we are happy with you in the good and pleasure you are deriving from it ... How about the parachute <u>you need one</u>?? ... *(Roger had said he didn't have one.)*

MAY 12, 1940. GRANDPA TO ROGER. (4 PAGES). EXCERPTS:
    .. Bill is fine and working intensely *(in medical school).* The professions of today are <u>tough</u>, and that is as it should be. The hard road is the way to success, that you have of course already learned. Tis a tough lesson but worthwhile. .. ❡ *In regard to Roger's ambition to enter another department, Grandpa can help when he comes in the summer but in the meantime:* ... <u>you</u> keep your eye and your <u>mind</u> on your job. My observation has been the many fail to obtain their objective because they have their minds elsewhere than on the job. <u>Let nothing</u> occupy your thoughts and your energies but your job and all pertaining thereto. This includes attention to your health — rest in sufficiency; play of the right sort enough to keep you mentally and physically alert; study even though it is only a little every day to keep your mind fit; physical recreation (recreation — get it?) daily to keep you psychically & physically alert. No destructive habits. Then no one can stop you. ... I go to Sheldon's Graduation on June 3 in Georgia. The lad has done well there. I am proud of him with all his handicaps.

MAY 20, 1940. ROGER TO GRANDPA. EXCERPT:
    I don't know how much newspaper propaganda can be trusted but it surely looks like England and France are in a very precarious situation. I have been trying but have not figured out what Germany might do were she to subjugate completely the Allies. In view of the part that the United States might play were Germany to win do you think, Dad, that I had better look to my military training again. As you know I did not attend camp last summer and so am that much behind those men who have. I have a feeling though that in case of hostilities it would not be long before I found myself in the air corps. If the government is really planning to build 50,000 airplanes yearly the demand for pilots is going to be very great.

JUNE 3, 1940. ROGER TO GRANDPA. EXCERPT:
    ... the U.S. Army is requiring every aircraft worker to furnish proof of U.S. citizenship. Do you suppose I could bother you to send a copy of my birth certificate as soon as possible.

JUNE 1940
Family travels for first visit with Roger since he left for California. Grandma, Sheldon, Akin and Vivian (to help with Akin, etc) to arrive mid June in Santa Monica for summer visit. Grandpa will travel by plane on July 13.
Roger's new apartment: 736 Via Somonte, Palos Verdes Estates, California.

JUNE 21, 1940. GRANDPA TO ROGER. EXCERPTS:
I had lunch with Mr. Spillsbury yesterday. There have been no further conversations between Mr. Hamilton *(vice-president at the Douglas plant)* and he as regards 66 *(the training department that Roger wishes to enter).* ¶ I explained to Mr. Spillsbury that you were in the Artillery Reserves and that in the event of mobilization you would probably be promptly called, as the Reserve Officers would be presumably. I told him that I felt you would prefer to remain at your work. He too felt that you would be of more service there than as a 2nd Lieutenant in the Artillery. I therefore asked him if he thought it wise and proper for you to go to Mr. Hamilton and state the situation and ask him if it might be his desire to place you on the list of those who were requested to remain at the plant. Mr. Spillsbury suggested that you state this is your life's work for which you have been preparing, that you have your own plane and that your heart is in aviation ... I feel that it would also be proper for you to say you are interested in 66 and would be glad to be considered for this position if in his opinion you are fitted for it ... I suggest also that you state that you are ready at any time to go to the colors if they need you for war service but you feel at this junction it might not be a necessity. That in an industry like airplane production you feel your services might be worth more to the country. Mr. Spillsbury thought it would be proper for you to do this now.. I leave to your own judgement, my son, and the calm excellent judgement of your Mother.. give this letter to her immediately upon her arrival.. Again I say to you that if you do not feel with me on this situation, do as you think best ...

JUNE 30, 1940. GRANDPA TO ROGER (6 PAGES). EXCERPTS:
Just before his trip to join the family and see Roger in California.
... Boy how I long to see you & grasp your hand and look straight into your dear honest eyes as man to man. You are a comfort & joy to me my boy my beloved son in whom I am well proud. Never another year shall pass that I do not see you. Life isn't worth that. My winter vacation shall be

spent with you God willing, hereafter ... ¶ Good luck and pleasant flying to El Paso ... wherever you are call on the ophthalmologist in that town & you will get assistance.

EARLY SEPTEMBER 1940
Grandpa, Akin and Sheldon drove back to Washington in their Packard. Grandma stayed to help Roger find and pay for "a nice place & proper arrangements." Grandma then went to visit Mrs. HasBrouck (Aunt Nettie) in San Francisco.

SEPTEMBER 3, 1940. ROGER TO GRANDPA. EXCERPTS:
I can truthfully say that I never spent a more delightful summer ... because I was living with the family. Dad, I enjoyed your company most of all. The long talks on subjects trivial and important and the good counsel you gave me concerning my life out here I appreciate very greatly. I do learn so much by talking to you. ¶ I surely get peeved at our government every once in a while because of the way it personally affects me. As you know the control of the air transportation of this country was taken from the independent CAA *(Civil Aeronautics Authority)* and placed under the Department of Commerce and many of the past leaders and advisors were removed. The latest is that the owner of any private plane must have the engine of the plane checked by a mechanic every 20 hours of flying time. That sounds good to a bunch of professors who do not see the practical application of such a regulation. *(He goes on to say that it creates financial hardships on present owners of planes who were already taking good care of their ships, that it will discourage the sale of private planes, and that present owners were finding ways to avoid such inspections.)*

SEPTEMBER 8, 1940. GRANDPA TO ROGER & RENÉE (9 PAGES). EXCERPT:
Uneventful trip back home, except I saw one of the prettiest girls en route from Nashville to Lexington KY, her home. Soft sweet voice, tall and slender as a swaying reed, gracious profile & high bred as an Arabian horse. I heard her say she was from Lexington & introduced myself & talked for a few minutes. She knew Alford & Laura and many others of my friends there ... ¶ .. I will get you the information on the Dart soon. One has to proceed with caution in Washington, 'The pussy footing center'.. Home looks good but <u>drab</u>; one misses so much the golden sunshine,

vivid colors, forbidding mountains & blue sea and all the rest of that gorgeous west ...

SEPTEMBER 15, 1940. GRANDPA TO GRANDMA (7 PAGES). EXCERPTS:

Dearest Mother, All's well. Have a pleasant visit in lovely San Francisco. Sheldon leaves for Chapel Hill; Bill & Helen for Baltimore Wednesday. Akin to St. Albans. Vivian has been a Saint & a Devil combined — as per usual. But has labored <u>so</u> hard for the boys. Sheldon particularly has been her care. She is trying so very hard to see that he has everything in order, particularly himself! ¶ How wonderful of you to find a home for Rog. Hope you found some one to look after him. *(Grandma helped Roger find a roommate, Herb.)* Good food is so essential to vigor & health. ¶ Didn't we have a wonderful summer with our boy! Thank you "mil gracias" for all you did ... Of my love for you sweetheart, dearest wife, companion, mother of my sons, it may only be measured by the span of my life and as far beyond that as I may project it. ¶ The British are having the H of the time but their <u>offensive</u> may save them. God grant it may. ¶ I shall send you the law — Selective Service Act — as soon as it is printed. You can then see just what we have to expect. It isn't bad. I somewhat doubt if Roger will be called. I am not certain in my mind what is best. It is a heroic time; our sons have the heroic natures. 'Tis no time for seeking shelter. They will not and that as it should be. Your and my duties are to back them up, strongly, courageously, unselfishly as becomes the mother & father of heroic youth. To keep the home fires burning; to make all the friends we can for them; to encourage and stimulate them to duty, honor & country. What a wonderful opportunity for them and for us. ...

Good night dearly beloved wife & mother, Devotedly, Dad

SEPTEMBER 15, 1940. GRANDPA TO ROGER (7 PAGES). EXCERPTS:

Dear Rog my son, Two weeks to the hour since I arrived here *(back from California)*. Boy has it been two full ones. ¶ We did have a nice summer did we not? It was a deep and abiding pleasure to be with you my son. I appreciate so much what you said in your letter. I feared I had been a bit of a bore in my talks with you. My hard experience taught me much that one does not learn from books and I just wanted you to have the advantage of it in so far as one may transfer experience. The basic laws of life are unfortunately not taught in our schools and universities. This results in the wrecking of many valuable lives. If I have been of use to you even though

I bored you at times my hard days will have not been in vain. ... ¶ I have not known friends to be harmful if one is sure they are. Yet one must be careful. Do not be too frank. Even with your most intimate friends, those in the plant in particular. One must always be watchful of jealousy where one may least expect it. Keeping one's own council isn't a bad idea. ... ¶ Hard work is mans greatest blessing son and I thank the dear Lord that I am permitted it. That I have the work and the strength to do it. The love of my dear family and the ability to help them — my greatest pleasure. I am a most fortunate person. *Sheldon leaves for University of North Carolina. Bill still in Baltimore medical school with Helen. Akin still lives at home and returns to St. Albans prep school in Washington.*

SEPTEMBER 22, 1940. GRANDPA TO ROGER (10 PAGES). EXCERPTS:

I appreciate your letter so much son and in particular what you said regarding my advice. I was afraid I had "preached" & possibly annoyed you. Whatever I may say or do dear son always remember love and affection prompt it though it may not always sound so. Your welfare lies nearest my heart and I cannot keep trying to pass on to you the result of experience harshly gained. It teaches one much that one may not learn from books. Also as Chaucer says "youth can outrun us but may not outwit us" old men for council. Daily exercise, clean thoughts and clean living, sufficient rest and daily study even though but ten minutes. Keep your mind on your work and keep that mind & the body that supports it fit. Of these are the elements of success & happiness and contentment. Cultivate those who are cultured and fine: they will usually be successful. Time is fleeting — do not waste it in the company of inferior people. Make your friends among such for your own spiritual, physical & mental good. 'Tis one of the rules of life to an intelligent person. ¶ What you say of Dept. 66 is welcome news. I cannot understand fully what the remarks meant. My reaction is this: they probably know you have plenty of 'pull' but have not chosen to use it and consequently mention this fact. Since you have not used any except in a <u>proper</u> way which doesn't really pull it provoked the remarks in your reports. I think you are wise in saying nothing further should be done at this time. I could bring pressure strong & direct but shall not do so unless & when you think it time. Follow up friends who are somebody and can help you. Why not son? Why not make friends of this sort? It is one of the axioms of life when properly done as you would do it. I do not mean to be a flunky. We cannot do that but good sense prompts one to be known among influential people. ¶ Hard work is what gives zest to life my dear son and I am glad to get back to it. Just as you would be after an absence from it. Those who do not have to work miss the best in life. I miss our lovely house on the bluff. It is a choice spot. If & when things assume normalcy we shall have a simple place in Palos Verdes where you can have home & we can visit you often. Cheerio for the future: you have great opportunities in which we shall glory in seeing you embrace. Fondest love dear son. Keep me as fully informed as you can.

Devotedly, Dad

SEPTEMBER 24, 1940
Roger's new apartment: 633 9th Street, Santa Monica, California.

SEPTEMBER 29, 1940. GRANDPA TO ROGER (15 PAGES). EXCERPTS:
.. What a lovely summer we had did we not? And how we did enjoy being with you dear son. We shall anticipate the same thing next year. If the conditions seem to warrant it we shall build a home in P. V. & spend all our vacations, winter & summer out there. That is a delightful thought to have isn't it? Let us treasure it as a thing to be hoped for in the near golden future. As you see Rog I am sold on Southern California Baja. Wasn't it wonderful of dear sweet mother to arrange your menage. That is love exemplified in deeds. May I tell you again something it took me a lifetime to learn. <u>Real</u> love seeks to <u>give</u> to the object of its affection; false love seeks to <u>take</u>, not give. Remember this, it will be of real value. You may judge friends, opponents, enemies, sweethearts et al by this rule to which there are few if any exceptions. Real love is unselfish; false love (& there is of course no such thing) is selfish. .. ¶ *(Grandpa responds to Roger's successful recruitment into the Dept. 66 training program, a responsibility in addition to Roger's normal timekeeping duties.)* ..it appears to me that they give most careful consideration to the selection of men for this place. This I admire since it means they intend to select from this group the future executives of the business hence they study them carefully. It takes from one to two years to learn the character of an employee. This I have learned from experience. The greater number of employees the longer it takes to know whether they have those qualities requisite for advancement to positions of trust. Hence watch your step not only in your work but in your private

life which by the way <u>isn't</u> private. You are under supervision <u>all</u> the time not by <u>direction</u> of your superiors. They inquire here, there, pick up information from this one, that one. Are you steady, are you sober, do you consort with harpies etc. etc. Not because of the moral altitude they may have but if you dissipate your energies after you leave the plant you <u>cannot</u> be good the next day — quite obvious and simple isn't it? I should say things look <u>very good</u> for you. Keep yourself physically fit by proper habits of life. This means daily exercise; it may be difficult but it can be done. Mentally fit, by daily good reading. Difficult but it can be done. Morally fit by association with people of the right sort. Avoid harpies, alcohol — a narcotic which lulls to sleep the guardian of your conscience — hard but it can be done. These are the rules which lead to the pinnacle of success. Not to observe them spells failure. Difficult, surely; 'tis the easy life that leads downward. The heights were and never will be easy. That is why they are isolated. Those of weak fiber who choose the pleasant easy way, who have not the good judgement to care for their physical, mental and moral welfare are destined to be <u>slaves</u> to those who are <u>superior</u> in these characteristics. This is quite obvious to you since you have a keen and discerning mind. The world is yours if you observe these rules. They are very <u>simple</u> as all great things are. ¶ (*Then to advise Roger of his extra duties and his new night shift — Grandpa had many times before been on night shifts in hospitals:*) As to the third shift: of course you can take it. Give it all you have. **Organize** your 24 hour day. So much time for sleep (take **no** drugs — **none**) Coffee, tobacco, Coca-Cola which is a drug. No "tablets" of any kind. Exercise to get physical fatigue — not to excess. This produces natural sleep. **Nothing** else does. Eat properly & <u>regularly</u>. **Rest enough**! 10 hours a day — **10 hours**. You need more rest under present conditions. A hot bath; a cold bath; food; a walk in the cold air. Read — something good, something silly ascending to which produces somnolence. Learn to relax; practice it. Relax your hands, your arms & legs; darken the room. Soon you can sleep but <u>don't take any medicine of any kind</u>. A week or so & you will conquer it. All of this I have been through hence I can advise you from personal experience and 40 years of professional observation. A swim in the ocean. A hard swim would do the trick. A stiff walk ... to produce <u>moderate</u> physical fatigue. Do your sleeping as much during the hours of darkness as you can. Split sleep is not as satisfactory but may be used as a substitute temporarily. ...

OCTOBER 3, 1940. ROGER TO GRANDPA. EXCERPTS:
He has taken his Dad's advice for how to deal with his extra duties and his new night shift — he sleeps 8–10 hours per day and eats heartily — he predicts that in another week that he will be accustomed to the new hours.

Do you know whether Vivian packed the Leica (camera) and had it sent back to Washington? I never saw it after she left ... ¶ The Douglas Aircraft Co. and the U. S. Government have finally succeeded in ousting all the operators from Clover Field in Santa Monica. I was out there this morning and felt very sad and very bitter against our government for being so stupid. These were the men who had given their lives to aviation and who had given at the same time to aviation the stimulus that put private flying in this country ahead of all other nations. Now these men are turned out with the consolation that they may return later when the emergency is over. In the meantime they will move from one crowded airport to another trying to hold their little capital interest. Under the most favorable conditions it is difficult for them to make ends meet, and before smooth sledding comes again many of them will be entirely ruined and disillusioned. The whole episode is very foolish and shortsighted. It is fortunate that I moved my ship *(plane)* to Mines Field. I don't like the field or the manner in which it is run, but at least I have a roof over the Dart. — *Grandpa wrote back,* I feel with you son as to the treatment of the air fields. It may be an object lesson to you how dumb & cruel is Government — all government, Yet there is another side. It is necessary in defense of our country, which means all you and I hold dear.

OCTOBER 5, 1940. GRANDPA TO ROGER (6 PAGES). EXCERPTS:
Indian Summer! Gorgeous colors. Mother, Akin and I had a grand ride this morning; warm sun & cool air & all the greens, reds, yellows with the lovely asters of every shade; the golden rod, iron weed & falling leaves. How we did wish for you dear son. ... When one works hard one needs to devote thought and time to the care of the machine. Just as when you fly a plane long distances, work it hard, it needs more care. ¶ Write every week Rog my son for Mother's sake. If it is just a post card or a collect telegram. It means so much to her; more than you can now realize. ... ¶ The war clouds thicken. Remember I am here & in a position to help you should the need come ... After the November elections things will happen fast; until then one may expect much babying and care of the poor "Selectees." After that

they will number among those not spoken of. I am happy in the thought that you are an officer. It means more than you can know ... I am doubtful if they will take you from the Air Corps industry. Either way son it will be to your advantage. You are well prepared for life no matter where you are called upon to function and this is a deep satisfaction to your mother and to me. If war does not dislocate you we shall build a simple home in Palos Verdes for you and for us, We will spend our winter and summer vacations there and you can have a place that you can call and feel home ... ¶ I am leaving tomorrow for Cleveland, Ohio to give two addresses at the academy of ophthalmology.

A LETTER FROM AKIN WAS ENCLOSED:

The woods have all or almost all turned red and yellow. Dad, Mother and I went on a beautiful ride this morning. My horse has never been taught how to place his feet and he stumbles all over the place. He never looks where he is going and will walk right into a tree. Last night Mother and I went to see "Spring Parade." It has probably been out for a month but it just got here. Dad didn't go because he had a bad cold.

Your brother, Akin

OCTOBER 13, 1940. GRANDPA TO ROGER (7 PAGES). EXCERPTS:

Am just back from Cleveland by plane. P.C.A. *(Pennsylvania Central Airlines)* has a non stop 2 hour flight!! Left there at 6:30 , Washington 8:25. Washington is becoming quite an air center, it will be one of the greatest in the U.S. & possibly the world..The new airport is on the river which is quite wide & roomy there ... ¶ Our drift is strongly towards war. The situation is complicated. It would appear that now is the time for us to strike in the Far East & settle that question. It should have been done 40 years ago. Our Navy can complete a drive out there that should settle the matters for several generations. I believe it the best thing to be done but not knowing all the facts judgement is difficult. ¶ Vivian has just returned from Vermont & Canada seeing her father & brothers. She found all satisfactory & so is at peace — <u>so she</u> says. You know Vivian & her peace — but her qualities of loyalty & devotion outweigh her faults so greatly that we are devoted to her. I think she has in mind us getting a place in Palos Verdes & she will remain there & take care of you and see us when we come out! She has fallen in love with California Baja which indeed all of us have.

Good night dear son: cheerio & may our dear Lord abide with you. Dad

OCTOBER 20, 1940. GRANDPA TO ROGER (8 PAGES). EXCERPTS:
... Whether you are called to the service for active duty will depend on what the plant requests. Do you wish me to do anything about it? ... I scarcely know what to advise but as we decided it would probably be best to let matters proceed without interference. *(He goes on to advise of some military friends in high places in California should the need arise.)* ¶ That we are preparing for <u>war</u> is sure. What will be extent cannot be said but it will be on an enormous scale. ¶ Dear son using your superior intelligence to offset your thoroughbred weaknesses, speaking physically, you will not be hurt by the night shift. Don't go from your dinner hour until far into the morning without <u>food</u>. I myself have passed through all of that. If you can't eat, <u>drink</u> and milk is the drink. Eat fruit, for what ails you along with the milk. Then for some daily exercise in the open. Teach yourself to walk; there is <u>no better</u> exercise. It has made the English nation vigorous. The lack of it here is very bad. ¶ *(Roger is a reserve officer.)* The army will call all reserves unless they are required in activities necessary to the national defense. It will be up to the Company (to ask for him to) remain as an essential employee. *(Grandpa gives Roger advice as to what to do if the Company does not ask to retain him, and whether he should be self-assertive and aggressive now.)* This I leave for your decision. It appears to me to be the time to act. 'Their comes a time in the affairs of men' etc. you know the rest. ¶ If you remain at Douglas we shall get a simple place in P. V. which will be home for you and for us also. I am feeling the corroding hand of time somewhat & a summer & winter rest is essential for Mother and I. Where so lovely as California Baja if you are there. *(Grandpa was 63 years old.)*

OCTOBER 27, 1940. GRANDPA TO ROGER (6 LONG PAGES). EXCERPTS:
He continues to prepare his son for meeting the challenges of a changing and uncertain world. He encloses newspaper clippings, one of which discusses a change in how the country will use its air power — the Army Air Corps will become the air force, a separate branch of our defense.
It is very reassuring. It makes the air force of immediate avail; relieves them of the duties of training, etc. etc. & leaves them as a mobile force ready for immediate action: a powerful weapon of defense <u>and offence</u>. The axiom of war; the best defense is offensive action. It heartens one to observe such evidence of policy in our military forces.. for the defense of our country and the Western Hemisphere. I have given much thought to your status but can

Company A, Hospital Corps, Army of Cuban Pacification, Havana, Cuba. Capt. William Thornwal

ing, top row center. (See page 30.)

see no reason changing our attitude. I rather find we are becoming a world power from a military standpoint and that we shall so continue throughout your generation & possibly longer, perhaps indefinitely. You remember I have said our influence (and the flag possibly) will fly from the arctic circle to Tierra del Fuego. You now see it in process of evolution. Power rules: 'tis a pity it is so but facts must be faced. Our military preparations indicate we will rule the Western World. We must do so in order to survive. Latin America is disunited & requires a strong hand to control it. Under that strong hand the Western World can dictate to the world both economically and militarily. The former is dependent upon the latter. Hence it will not be disadvantageous for you to be called to the colors. The lads who have a good military background will have the upper hand in your time. Of this I am quite sure though there may be some slips here and there. In the long run it will tell. Again service with our forces will lead to wide travel & a larger horizon which will be of the same benefit to you as mine has been to me. I do not mean for you to go in for military service casting other things aside but only to show that should you be called there are opportunities that will be of value because you will be in a position <u>to take advantage</u> of them in view of your education. In this end keep yourself fit physically & mentally ... read military history & the biographies of military leaders & thus broaden your knowledge & your mind. Do not sink to the level of the average American whose education both physical and mental ceases upon his graduation. Have a care of your habits, exercise, food, rest, & the narcotics of civilization <u>and</u> its moral degeneracy. Right is right & wrong is wrong & there can be no compromises. ¶ Keep me fully informed dear son of any developments in the plant or the Service that I may plea at your disposal for consideration my experience so that you may use it should you consider it of value. ¶ I am proud & happy that you have solved a really important problem in your life — "How to Live." You will need this throughout your span on Earth. I see so many who have built a success & cannot participate in it because of the failure of health at the crucial time because of lack of care of themselves earlier in life. A man may live vigorously, mentally & physically to 75 yrs. if he will. If he wills it so & so lives in consonance with love of health & good common sense. You give evidence of being able to accomplish this. Remember the lesson that our darling mother has taught by precept & example. You will live long in the hand thy God giveth thee. ... My letters to you are private: destroy or lock them up.

NOVEMBER 3, 1940. ROGER TO GRANDPA. EXCERPTS:
Anginette HasBrouck has just passed away.

Mom telephoned me Saturday from San Francisco and told me about Aunt Nettie. I am very sorry that she was not able to arrive in time. But maybe it was for the best; it would have been very hard on her if it had been necessary for her to spend any amount of time in San Francisco. I received a wire tonight saying that she would arrive in Los Angeles Thursday morning. It will be wonderful to see her again ... ¶ At this time it looks like Roosevelt is in again (for a third term as president). It worries me; I don't trust the man or the administration. I only hope that Roosevelt and his cohorts are not of a mind to make the United States Government a dictatorship of one man or a small group of men. I have been in very close contact with the workmen here in the plant for over a year now and have come to know them quite well in many respects. The vast majority of them support Roosevelt and his program as it is advertised, but they are for the most part good patriotic Americans. They may be fooled for a short while but if it comes to a real test I believe the country is safe in their hands. About the laboring class in the remainder of the country I know nothing, but I trust that the class is uniform throughout ... *Roger thinks it might be best if he could be transferred to the Air Corps Reserve and asks his father whether this is possible.*

NOVEMBER 10, 1940. GRANDPA TO ROGER AND RENÉE (16-PAGE LETTER), EXCERPTS:
.. We *(Grandpa and Mr. Spillsbury, family friend and Douglas Aircraft executive)* were in accord in thinking you would be more valuable to our country in your present position than in the army ... Your conception of it *(the service)* and my experience in it are widely different dear son. It is <u>not</u> as you picture it ... if Douglas asks you to remain you will probably be kept there ... hundreds of young men who are capable of being officers in the artillery & air corps who have not your technical training in <u>production</u> which is now the most important item in National Defense. If and when you are called we can arrange the transfer to the air corps. However son I would not allow enthusiasm in flying tempt you into the most hazardous avocation in all the world. Remember the future years of your life. To put it very starkly I think you are much too superior for such work. Also I think you have not the neuro-muscular set up for the military flying. You will

probably acquiesce in this summation of your powers ... To take you out in the middle of your training would not be to the best interests of the service. *(Grandpa tries to make a parallel here with Roger's brother, Bill, who is finishing his medical school training before going into the Army Medical Corps. He then asks Roger to give it careful thought.)* ... If Mr. H makes this request *(to stay on his present job)* <u>then</u> I am in a position to help you. I have friends in the War Dept. that can be of great help after such a request is made. Confer with Mother *(she is visiting)* and then wire or phone me what your decision is *(so Grandpa can tell Mr. Spillsbury to initiate the request)*. This opinion is subject to your own. It is a crises in your life; give it careful study <u>now</u>, at once ... time is now here for prompt action. It means everything to your future ... Use no names in your wire. If you wish to talk with me call me on the telephone at my expense. Money is no object when such a decision is to be made ... *(we do not)* wish for you to evade your duty to country but in the confusion of today the individual is lost in the immensity of the scene ... It touches me deeply that my son should have such noble and prophetic thoughts. It touched Mr. Spillsbury too. Your letter is fine and with an understanding far beyond your years — you have an old head on your shoulders. May our dear Lord save you for the future good of family & country.

Darling Mother, I am enclosing Roger's letter. I have read it at least a dozen times. It is a wonderful document and I prize it highly. Return it to me by mail forthwith and at once ... Good night my beloved ones. These be heroic & difficult days but out of them we shall emerge stronger for the trial. Be of good heart & brave courage. We shall meet the necessities of the hour with fortitude & success. Happy are we that we have four splendid sons, a home with pure love & quiet affection, unselfish devotion to one another. Good friends, complete confidence in the loyalty of us all, unselfish devotion. These are the <u>finest</u> things that life offers & we have it in abundance thanks be to a wonderful wife and mother whom we adore. So cheerio, all will be well.

Your devoted husband and father

November 10, 1940. Grandpa to Roger (5 pages). Excerpts:
Asking him to give careful thought to coming home for Christmas.

Mother is speeding home on the stream liner. I judge she is crossing Wyoming tonight. She is due here at 8:30 Wednesday morning. I shall meet her. I want to fill the house with flowers & have all cheer possible for her. She is sad at leaving quite the apple of her eye and at losing her last beloved relative *(Anginette HasBrouck).* ¶ There are things that you and I should discuss that have much to do with your future. My lack of education I admit is a handicap in but cold experience with men & circumstances permit me an experience which thank God you have not had to deal with. This hard & practical experience may be of value to you. *(Roger flies home for Thanksgiving instead of Christmas.)* ¶ I am getting a copy of a Thesis Dr. Graham wrote in 1822* for his graduation in medicine at the Transylvania University in Lexington, KY. Shall send you a copy. It is well for you to know you have ancestry of education & culture. The aristocracy of America, that is what bears you up in time of stress. See to it that you do not dissipate it in your progeny. You get me! ¶ Akin ... so much like you my dear son in his steadiness, considerations, performance of duty. You two are a source of great happiness to darling Mother and me.

He enclosed a letter written to him from Helen. Among his comments: She doesn't drink & she doesn't smoke. It means more than you yet realize. The mother of your children shouldn't do this son. It means a weakness of <u>character</u>. No I am not old fashioned. Times change but principles & character do not.

December 2, 1940. Roger to Grandpa. Excerpt:
His Dept. 66 training program has been discontinued — his training will now be in several departments and more comprehensive.

I will do sheet metal work, hand forming, riveting, welding, etc. and am not to be transferred from a department until I am accomplished in its work. This type of training will take several years but when and if I finish will <u>know</u> the complete background of aircraft construction, and should have no trouble in the Sales Department. *(The Douglas Chief of Material later tells Grandpa by letter, "He will be transferred to a given shop department followed by subsequent transfers to other departments on the same basis on a long-term plan that will enable him to acquire a thorough knowledge of the business on a 'doing' basis rather than just observing on a quick student tour. This, I believe is one of the very best of student training arrangements worked out for anyone to date.")*

---

*Christopher Columbus Graham was Grandpa's great grandfather. His M.D. thesis was entitled "Morbid Sympathy and Excitement."

December 15, 1940. Grandpa to Roger (14 pages), Excerpts:
Enclosed are recent newspaper articles: one (which turned out to have been entirely false) purports to describe two attempts by the Germans to invade England from the French coast, thwarted mostly at sea by British bombs, with some 80,000 German troops perishing in the attempts, reports of mutinies in the German army, troops declaring that they would not again face the "burning sea" in a third invasion attempt. Grandpa tells Roger he had learned about this two months ago. From letter:

. . . Uncle Bob's letter which you will be interested in. Also General Fiekels. You will make time to call so don't defer it too long. They are sweet simple people & will be friends and advise you, assist you. 'Tis an opportunity to make <u>friends</u>, real friends. ¶ ... In my opinion the U. S. is due for a long war: possibly lasting a generation or more. In this I may be in error. No one can say. Having training in artillery plus air training will fit you for rapid advancement. This is one side of the picture. The adverse is the gamble on the war lasting so long & leaving you among the stranded when it is over. The <u>hazard</u> of military training in the air; the long time of service; the isolation from civil life. It is a knotty problem. Give it study and careful thought. Yours is the decision dear son, ours only to assist you. Whatever your decision may be we are back of you. The sky being the limit ... Remembering our darling Mother & her great love for you. Not to weaken your decision for she has the courage of Olympus and the fortitude of the God's thereon; but to strengthen this decision & make it based upon duty, love and devotion to our beloved Mother & the Nation & last but not least your own future. One must have a care for ones self too. ¶ ... your new work ... intriguing.. In those activities which entail hazards be careful. Welding is dangerous to eyes from the ① intense light. You have a powerful lens in your eyes which focuses the light in the retina. The ultra violet & the infra red, <u>invisible</u> to our eyes is the most dangerous. Special glasses are necessary. I will send them to you. ¶ ② Another hazard to eyes is at the lathe: metal or wood. Many have lost an eye at such work. A particle of metal or other foreign substance may penetrate the globe & usually destroys the eye. Guard your eyes carefully — most carefully. Anything you require in this work write me & I will send it to you. *(Grandpa often reminded his sons of the importance of protecting their eyes.)* Also dear son have a care for the saboteurs; they are everywhere. ¶ We have been concerned as to the flue in California; sunny California! Should you be ill go to the hospital at once. Phone Dr. Spires. Never mind the cash. Mother and Dad will see to that and with great joy & satisfaction. What is money compared to the safety & comfort of our loved ones. Against this it has no value ... ¶ .. Budget your day. Systematize it. So much for work, so much for play. One must play in ones own way. So much in open air & sunshine. So much for reading and study. So much for rest. It is such men who succeed. Using intelligence in the distribution of their energies. See that your play is elevating in character and not spent in waste of health and energy & morals. I might say that the playtime of a mans life spells success or failure. Care as to the night school, you have a fine education and I doubt if you require night school. *(Roger had mentioned in a letter that he thought it might be necessary for him to go to night school to obtain knowledge of the departments he would be sent to.)* You are quite capable of outlining your own course & do your own study. This will be of much greater value to you than to <u>be</u> taught. It is the great failure of our youth that they think they must <u>be</u> taught. Why not study yourself? You thus get the information you require plus the mental discipline and training plus the rest. I suggest you do it this way. You can get from the school all the information as to the outline; obtain the books and do your own studying. I assure you it will be of greater value to you than coaching. If you require a modicum of the latter well & good, obtain it. Give a care to rest, to health, to proper play. You are on a lifetime job. Why hurry. The old saws are still good, "the more haste the less speed." Conserve you health bodily, mentally and morally. It will serve you well. Bless you my son. I know your good sense will guide you. I have seen so many youths burn themselves out working all day & going to night school. I doubt its value.

DECEMBER 28, 1940. ROGER TO GRANDPA. EXCERPTS:
    It was certainly marvelous to talk to you on the telephone last Thursday. I am only sorry I missed Sheldon and Akin, but I was thinking of them anyway. The call took less than five minutes to put through and really made things so much easier than it would have been on Christmas day when both of us would have spent three or four hours waiting around the telephone. ¶ .. missed so much not being in Washington ... but Christmas day Herb *(room-mate)* and I flew to his ranch for dinner and had a very enjoyable time.

JANUARY 5, 1941. ROGER TO GRANDPA. EXCERPTS:
He continues to move from one department to another — so far, welding,

sheet metal, riveting and sub-assembly. — *he manually performs and becomes skilled in all he is taught.*

I like this assembly work the best. It is not the most difficult by any means and the men are not paid very much, but it is here that the airplane first begins to take on a recognizable shape, such as — bomb doors, pilots seats and supports, etc. ❡ Dad, don't forget to let me know if you find anything about my being called into military service. I have the Dart for sale but am not trying very earnestly to get rid of it. However, if you find that I shall probably be called I will have to work fast and hard so I won't have it left on my hands.

JANUARY 19, 1941. GRANDPA TO ROGER (9 PAGES). EXCERPTS:
... I enclose Kennedy's talk (Joseph Kennedy: 'Don't Enter War'); it should go down in history as comparable to General Washington's farewell address and Lincoln's Gettysburg speech. ❡ *Refers to tomorrow's Inauguration Day (Roosevelt's third term) as a Roman Holiday. He says Bill & Sheldon are sick but:* "Your Dad is OK. Sound as a nut ... at 64 ... expect to be warning folks for a decade. Just so long as I can serve those I love well and diligently I want to be around. ❡ *Reminds Roger not to delay calling upon a general and his wife who Grandpa has told about Roger. Just another of the many family friends and potentially helpful contacts in the Santa Monica vicinity which Grandpa has been giving Roger over the last year.* ❡ Cheerio son: rest, proper food, some exercise & sunshine daily — make it possible. Keep yourself mentally & physically & morally fit and the world is yours.

Ever & always, Devotedly, Dad

JANUARY 23, 1941. GRANDPA TO ROGER (14 PAGES).
Many reserve officers are being called to active service — he continues to speak to his military friends (mostly Generals and Colonels) and to executives at Douglas about how to defer Roger's active duty (by placing his name at the bottom of the call list) until he finishes his training at Douglas — tells Roger what he needs to do and who he should contact to best plead his case for completing his training (this includes the Reserve Corps commander in the San Francisco area who Grandpa's General friend has spoken to about Roger). It is an extensive network of people from whom Grandpa has procured information, advice and action on Roger's behalf. Grandpa advises Roger to act promptly because after Roger is ordered to duty "nothing can be

done." Tells Roger to keep him advised.

JANUARY 26, 1941. GRANDPA TO ROGER (10 PAGES). EXCERPTS:
Renée has come home from a stay in the hospital after serious stomach sur-
gery — now convalescing — Grandpa had spent all of his time away from
the office with her).

Mother dear is doing splendidly. Downstairs & walking about & looks
entirely her dear self again. She can laugh again without a hurt in her stomach. She sends her fondest love to you. It is snowing heavily and has been
doing so since one o'clock, several inches deep now ... keep it up throughout
the night. Mother sits in her easy chair near to me as I write, reading and
enjoying herself and I am enjoying looking at her and having her dear presence near me. ¶ *(She will come visit Roger when able to travel.)* Later I can
fly out. I don't fly in the east in the winter. It is too uncertain and hazardous, both as to time, fatigue and life. Do you realize that your Dad is in his
65th year? I don't, but I must consider it in the matter of fatigue. ¶ Bill has
recovered *(from flu)*, having exams ... Sheldon I think is coming along. Sheldon is ---- Sheldon ... Akin quick, steady & doing well. Now that all is well
with my beloved family I too am happy and content. Were I called to cross
the Great Divide at any time I could do so with peace in my heart. ... ¶ The
week beginning July 3rd will be a strenuous one. Aviation course, and a lot
of things I have to go to at night, not social but hospital Board meetings and
the like. Will be home every night <u>this</u> week. I wish you would call us this
week and report what has taken place in your efforts. The ground work has
been done here. All I can do through people in a position to be an 'all out'
help to you has been done. It is now up to you; carry it out promptly and I
know you can efficiently. It is one of those times son when <u>action</u> is necessary. Go to it. <u>Keep in touch with me.</u> We can place you on the deferred list:
you can complete your period of training; <u>then</u> (your superior) can write to
the War Dept. <u>here</u> and you can be put in the "War Dept. Pool" ... *(then with*
your training) be given a position of sufficient importance ...

FEBRUARY 1, 1941. ROGER TO GRANDPA.
He started a night school one-year course in Aircraft Drafting — he needed
the training and no other way to get it. He has learned that he had been
deferred until April and asks his Dad what he thinks about how to proceed.
Had lunch with General and Mrs. Fickel (friend of Grandpa's).

FEBRUARY 4, 1941.
War Department disapproved a request by Douglas Aircraft for Dad's transfer to the "War Department Reserve Pool."

FEBRUARY 10, 1941. ROGER TO GRANDPA.
Now in Dept. 13, Final Assembly.

FEBRUARY 19, 1941. ROGER TO GRANDPA. EXCERPT:
He continues to make his deferment pleas to the people Grandpa has advised.
    Sunday I finished overhauling the Dart. I put in new rings, ground the valves and gave it a general cleaning ...

MARCH 6, 1941.
Mailed by Grandpa to Roger and Renée. Telegrams, etc., concerning Roger's deferment.

MARCH 10, 1941. ROGER TO GRANDPA EXCERPTS:
His Mom visiting. He has been transferred to Dept. 27, Production Control.
    Dad, it begins to look like the army matter is finally straightening out. I have you to thank for it and really appreciate all of the time and effort you spent. ¶ Sunday afternoon I flew through Cajon Pass to Victorville to try to sell my airplane. For the first time in weeks I flew in perfectly clear weather. The cumulus clouds were beautiful and the air was cool and crisp. While going thru the pass I flew quite close to Old Baldy covered with snow. The snow was so deep that no trees were visible for almost a third of the distance down its sides. It reminded me of Switzerland and was most beautiful. I hope before long that you can make a trip like that with me.

MARCH 13, 1941. GRANDPA TO ROGER AND RENÉE (5 PAGES). EXCERPTS:
    ... We are carefully keeping your letters for you when we pass on. They will be a journal that will prove of value both personally and historically. These be historic times. ¶ Your description of the flight through Cajon Pass was fascinating. Aren't we happy that you are in your job until September? ¶ It is snowing again this morning & more promised for today & night & colder. Glad Mother darling that you are out of it. It will be April when you come back and Spring. Take care of yourself & stay in the sunshine & get daily exercise. See what contacts you can make for Roger & us in the sum-

mer *(family will visit again).*

MARCH 24, 1941. ROGER TO GRANDPA. EXCERPTS:

I imagine Mom wrote you that we spent last weekend with the Boones after having lunch with General and Mrs. Fickel *(General Fickel had been a great help in the long process of Roger's military deferment).* Capt. Boone* seemed quite well except that he was quite nervous and restless. I slept in the same room with him and noticed that his sleep was anything but restful. During the night he yelled 'help' in his sleep so loud that I almost jumped out of bed. He continued to shout so I had to shake him several times to quiet him. I do wish that he would take several weeks leave and just relax for the whole time. *(Grandpa wrote about Capt. Boone in his next letter, "Sad news you write me regarding Capt. Boone. I fear the future looks dark for him unless he can and will take a good rest. There is much that does not appear on the surface. A fine man with a splendid record.")* ¶ *(Still in Production Control, will be transferring soon to Dept. 33, Material Control)* I am just now beginning to realize what a complicated and integrated affair any big business is. And because of the tremendously rapid expansion demanded of the airplane manufacturers I can easily understand why so many bottlenecks have been encountered and why progress seems to be so slow.

MARCH 28, 1941. LETTER TO ROGER (8 PAGES). EXCERPTS:

I would suggest cultivating the army in & about L.A., Santa Monica, etc. ¶ I think I wrote you about our contemplated trip to Yosemite in the high Sierras. Want you to be with us. Remember this son: holidays are not luxuries, they are necessities. Going without them is poor judgement & advances you not at all in the long run.

APRIL 9, 1941. ROGER TO GRANDPA.

Roger still thinking about the uncertainty of how close the U.S. is to war. If

---

*Captain Boone (Joel Thompson Boone, August 2, 1889 – April 2, 1974) was a United States Navy officer who received the Medal of Honor for his actions during WWI, later received the Army's Distinguished Service Cross and was awarded the Silver Star six times, making Boone the most highly decorated medical officer in the history of the U.S. armed services. Eventually moving back to Washington, he was a close family friend until his death. He was White House physician to six presidents. Roger's two sons, Bob and Roger, knew him from the Carabao Wallows. See photo on following page.

Joel T. Boone. This picture was framed and hung in the Davis household. Inscription: "To the House of Davis where love and hospitality abound to refresh one's soul. 1939. Joel T. Boone US Navy."

war comes he wants to be in the Air Corps. When to request acceptance into the Air Corps looms.

APRIL 21, 1941. ROGER TO GRANDPA. EXCERPTS:
Roger flew to Phoenix and El Paso over the weekend to see family friends.
... The Dart's engine never missed a beat. ¶ I don't think you understood me quite correctly, Dad, in my views towards joining the Air Corps. What I meant was that if war comes and I were called to service, not if I were called in peacetime, I would prefer to do my best to enter the Air Corps. The time of service would be the same in any branch of army during war. Concerning the War Dept. Pool, though, I also feel that prompt action would be best as conditions are still growing darker.

APRIL 24, 1941. RENÉE TO ROGER (9 PAGES). EXCERPTS:
Speaks about Grandpa's course on aviation medicine, looming darkness of war, the Pool and Roger's deferment proceedings, then comments:
In thinking things over perhaps it would be just as well for you <u>not</u> to ask Barbara Douglas *(we believe she was the daughter of the president of Douglas Aircraft, Donald Douglas)* for a date — that is not <u>now</u>. I think it might be better to wait until after the request had been made *(the second request for his deferment by Douglas Aircraft).* ¶ These past two weeks Washington has been crowded with people — good for the merchants but hard on the inhabitants. First the Cherry Blossom crowd — then the D. A. Rs. *(Daughters of the American Revolution)* and now the Red Cross. ¶ Here's to a happy summer for us all in California. I don't know yet whether Bill & Helen will go ... undecided. ... We are undecided what to do about Sheldon. He is at the baulky age and filled with his own ideas — all of which is natural. This June is going to find his studies in a mess but he <u>will</u> not be dropped. The University *(of North Carolina)* is very lenient the first year and then to his advisor is bully for him and rather taking most of the blame for the first quarter upon his own shoulders ... The dearest love to you, Rog Boy, Affectionately, Mother

APRIL 29, 1941. ROGER TO GRANDPA. EXCERPT:
Jim Farra, supervisor of the Sales Department, has offered Roger a job and Roger's current boss is making all possible for Roger's transfer in a month, cutting his current training a little short.
... I have just passed the 200 hours mark in my flying time and feel very

proud of myself ... I am no authority on flying but I feel that I am no longer an amateur.

MAY 9, 1941. ROGER TO GRANDPA. EXCERPT:

It just doesn't seem possible that two more months will see us together again at Palos Verdes. How time does fly. By the time you all arrive out here I will have been working for Douglas for two years. At times I think I have progressed very well during those two years, but I look around me to see others who have done just as well <u>or</u> much better. Then I realize that the further one goes ahead the more difficult it is to continue because the field narrows and everyone you compete with is out to do the same thing you are." *Now in Dept. 7, Procurement Follow-Up. He continues to work on getting Sheldon summer employment at Douglas.*

MAY 10, 1941. ROGER TO GRANDPA. EXCERPTS:

Tomorrow morning I start to work in the Sales Dept. at last. It has been a long time that I have wanted just this, but now 'it is only the beginning, only the beginning'. in view of this job I am getting in Sales it seems to me that little will be accomplished by waiting any longer before writing to get me placed in the Reserve Poll. It will have to be done before next September and by that time I am certain my status in the Sales Dept. will <u>not</u> have been changed ... Monday night I went to Field Artillery Class held in L. A. ¶ Herb and I flew to San Francisco over last weekend. We visited some friends of his over Saturday night and had a very gay time ... The wind was blowing quite briskly from the north during the whole weekend so it took us 4 hrs. 35 mins. to go up, <u>but</u> it only took 3 hrs. 25 mins. to return. Quite some difference in time.

MAY 11, 1941. GRANDPA TO ROGER (5 PAGES). EXCERPTS:

Mother dear was so pleased at your thought for her today and I am so happy that you thought of her. It is such apparently little things that make others happy and so make you happy too. ¶ There is much remarkable development in Akin these last two months. He has reached the age of development from boyhood to young manhood. He is doing well in his studies and applies himself assiduously. The same steady good student you were. He is so much like you in so many ways. I call him Rog about half the time. ¶ The work at the office very heavy and I am putting in very long and heavy days so that I am a bit fogged. Vacation is in sight however and the thought of the vacation in Southern California with you is cheering. ... ¶ The situation in our country grows more confused and dangerous. The people have no leader & dangerous situations face us on all sides. It is a condition that makes every thoughtful person anxious and concerned. Do not let the pressing duties of the day keep you away from the rules of life son. Some study, exercise outside, sufficient rest, clean play. Make those habits fixed while you are young. Fondest love from us all dear boy.

Devotedly, Dad

MAY 28, 1941. ROGER TO GRANDPA. EXCERPT:
I listened to the President's speech last night and was amazed at the lack of detailed information he divulged. It seemed clear to me though that he meant to stop at <u>nothing</u> in order to help England. Maybe he is correct and maybe he is not. Personally, I believe we should arm ourselves to the limit and fortify South America and all the islands in the Atlantic and to H--- with Hitler. But regardless of who is right we have to stick together. The proximity of war makes me think of the War Dept. Reserve Pool again. As I said in my last letter I don't believe that the time to act will ever be more appropriate than it is now, at least not for a long while. If there is no possibility of it going through please let me know at once so I can start for the Air Corps. The way I look at it is that if I go into the Army at all it will be for the duration of the war anyway because I am sure we will be in it, and if I have to be in for the duration I would much rather be in the Air Corps. Sure I stand to lose more, <u>but</u> I also stand to gain more, much more.

JUNE 1, 1941. GRANDPA TO ROGER (5 LONG PAGES). EXCERPTS:
Thanks Roger for his telegram while on his trip to Salt Lake City. He continues to work through his friends on Roger's behalf.
.. I feel just as you do about the war situation and the President. I have yet to hear him make a speech that had any weight to it. This last one bears an awful let down. We expected <u>something</u>. ... no reason for you to take any action regarding the Air Corps. May I ask you to consult with me before doing so. For dear mother's sake please accede to my request ... I do not think it by any means assured that you would be in the army for the duration. The idea is to build up a large force of trained Reserves and pass them back into civil life. For this reason I think it would be better if you went

into the artillery where there would be every possibility of your release at the end of one year. You could then hold your job I am sure. Through Mr. Cover, General Pratt, etc. etc. we could accomplish this I am sure. You now have a good start and it would be a pity to lose what we have worked so hard to obtain. If you went into the Air Corps it would mean years before you could get out. ... There are many developments and the country is not prepared to plunge into war. Germany is anxious to avoid a conflict with us at this time as is Japan. Don't base your conceptions on the Presidents speech. His speeches mean less than nothing. Hence I ask you to proceed with caution & deliberation. ..I am sure that with your excellent good sense you will see the wisdom of all of this. ¶ Bill will be through *(medical school)* in 2 more years & as things look now will go directly into the service as 1st Lt. Medical Reserve Corps. He can get his internship in a military hospital. ¶ We are counting the days until we see you *(Grandpa has rented a house in Palos Verdes starting July 1st for the summer)*. I anticipate so much pleasure in discussing sundry & various things with you.

ENCLOSED WAS A LETTER FROM AKIN. EXCERPT:

I have just made quite an addition to my collection. One of my friends found a whole chest full of knives from the Philippines in his basement and sold sixteen of them to me for thirteen dollars. Several have silver ornaments on their handles.

JUNE 6, 1941. ROGER TO GRANDPA. EXCERPTS:

... have had a full week ... quite tired from my (weekend) trip ... My trip to Salt Lake was very enjoyable and interesting. The weather was clear and smooth from here to Las Vegas (253 mi). However from Las Vegas on to Salt Lake (363 mi) the air, even though very clear, was very bumpy and the Dart tossed around like a cork in a choppy sea. Needless to say the boy with me became air sick and the quart container I have had in the plane for over a year came in handy. I did not feel the bumpy air at all so it looks like I am getting the better of the air sickness which used to hit me once in a while last year ... At Salt Lake City we spent most of the time browsing around looking at such things as the Mormon Temple, State Capital, the University, etc. Saturday afternoon we went out to the lake to go swimming but a cold wind was blowing so hard that all we did was taste the water to see if it really was <u>salty</u> — ugh! ... ¶ Dad, don't worry about my taking any steps towards the Air Corps without first consulting you. ¶ *He continues to work on helping Sheldon secure a summer job at Douglas.* ¶ Mom, do you remember that when you were out here last we agreed to diminish my check from home by the amount of any future raises I received? Well, I just received a raise of $5.00 per week so my check can be diminished $20.00.

JUNE 6, 1941. ROGER TO GRANDPA. EXCERPTS:
I'll write my letter this week from Phoenix as that is where I am at the moment. It seems that I get the "wanderlust" almost every weekend now ... ¶ I know you read about all the trouble at the North American Aviation Plant (across the street from El Segundo Douglas). From my window I was able to see the whole affair. No matter what the papers say and no matter what we might think personally of the Army's taking over private property, the job was well done. At exactly nine o'clock in the morning the Army moved in from three directions, not at all in a hurried manner but slowly and methodically with machines, etc. unlimbered directly behind. In half an hour the crowd had been moved back a quarter of a mile on all sides. The few who were hurt were those who just refused to move when several hundred soldiers pushed over them.

JUNE 10, 1941. LETTER FROM DONALD W. DOUGLAS (PRESIDENT OF DOUGLAS AIRCRAFT) TO THE OFFICE OF THE UNDER SECRETARY OF WAR.
Gentlemen, On December 28, 1940, this company requested a reconsideration of your refusal of transfer to the War Department Reserve Officers Pool of 2nd Lt. Roger H. B. Davis, FA-Res. On January 9th, 1941, your office again regretted their inability to approve this transfer stating that his case would be given 'to agency responsible for determining the period of deferment which may be granted to this officer'. The Office of the Commanding General, Headquarters Ninth Corps Area, Presidio of San Francisco, under date of January 7/1941 gave notice that deferment would be granted to April 7, 1941. On March 4, 1941, this company requested his deferment extended to September, 1941 as he was engaged in a work program that would not be completed until about that Time. In a letter from Ninth Corps area under date of March 11, 1941 permission was granted for deferment to September 1, 1941. ¶ This man started with this company on July 6, 1939 in the position of Timekeeper. His work showed exceptional promise and he was given several merit increases. The early part of December, 1940 he was picked by one of our Executives as a man of outstanding ability and placed in our Stu-

dent Engineering Group where he was given a shop training course leading toward a better understanding of the methods and procedures of shop practice, thereby enabling him to qualify for assignments of greater scope and responsibility. His training program was completed on May 22, 1941, and he was placed in the Parts Sales Department handling sales releases. This work embodies the breaking down of company orders, the greater part of which are for planes built for the United States Army, Navy and Marine Corps and the Royal Air Force of Great Britain, for spare parts and assemblies into their proper component parts and then writing up the shop orders for proper routing and distribution throughout the various departments of the shop concerned with the manufacturer. To be able to do this, the individual must have a thorough knowledge of the shop, its departments and what is done in each, to enable him to properly issue and complete the work assigned to him. ¶ As a result of this training and his exceptional ability he has become a very valuable man to the production and rapid delivery to the Governmental agencies of spare parts and assemblies. ¶ The Douglas Aircraft Company is operating its main plant in Santa Monica at capacity, turning out principally bombers for the United States Army Air Corps and the British Government. Its El Segundo division is building a substantial quantity of dive bombers for the U.S. Navy. We have Army Air Contracts for substantial quantities of light bombers, observation and cargo airplanes which are to be constructed in a new plant at Long Beach. California, which will be completed within a few months. The ground was broken a few weeks ago by your Corps of Engineers for a Government assembly plant in Tulsa, Oklahoma, which is to be operated by this company as an assembly plant for the assembly of Army B-24 Heavy Bombardment Airplanes. The resultant necessary expansion of personnel resulting from this tremendous increase in production makes obvious the indispensability of key personnel such as Mr. Davis. ¶ Upon consideration of the facts set forth above it is hoped that before any hasty decision is made, full cognizance be given to Mr. Davis' qualifications and position with this company, emphasizing their connection with the work being carried on under the National Defense Program and grant him an indefinite transfer to the War Department Reserve Officers Pool.

JUNE 22, 1941. ROGER TO GRANDPA. EXCERPTS:
.. just returned from Susie's wedding (the Boones' daughter) and a weekend with the Boones. ... The Boone's feelings were the same as mine.

They wanted the whole Davis family to be there ... Fortunately everything ran smoothly. It was a good thing too because Joel was very tired and very nervous and had the plans gone awry the increased excitement might not have gone well with him. ¶ .. I like my job more and more as the time goes on ... Every day my job takes me all over the plant and I am able to add to the knowledge I gained while in Dept. 66.. ¶ I suppose all of you, like everyone else in the world, is wondering just what the outcome of Germany's declaring war on Russia will be. A few of the naval officers at San Diego ventured the opinion that Russia would fall in a short while and under the thumb of Germany might seize the Aleutian Islands and Alaska. If that should happen we would be encircled, by the world in fact. Then again, other officers felt that Russia was too big to conquer and that after reaching the wheat and oil fields Germany would go no further and by that time Russia would be willing to make peace. In either event the position of the United States would be weakened. Let us all hope, however, that Germany has bitten off more than she can chew in this new war of hers.

JULY–AUGUST 1941.
Grandpa, Grandma, Bill, Helen, and Akin summer vacation with Roger in California. Sheldon made other plans. Roger sublets his place for the summer and lives with the family at their rented home in Palos Verdes.

AUGUST 1941. EXCERPT:
Roger is transferred to the Officers Reserve Pool of the War Department (meaning that his call to active service is indefinitely postponed and only the Secretary of War himself can call him to service). From a letter to his friend Cabell Maddox dated August 8, 1941:

I now have my chance in the aircraft industry and am out to make the most of it. I finally landed my job in the Sales Department and believe I shall remain there a long time. I like to work and think there are some excellent opportunities. Sometimes, though, I envy the life you are leading and wish that I could be serving the country in a more direct capacity.

SEPTEMBER 6, 1941. ROGER TO GRANDPA. EXCERPT:
... We had such a wonderful summer together. The time passed all to quickly, but we owe every hour we had together to you, Dad *(for making it all possible).*

September 13, 1941. Roger to Grandpa. Excerpts:
Raise given to all Douglas employees. Roger's was $4 per week making his weekly salary $39. He is not a "union man" so his raise was less than what most others received.

I think I have decided to turn the Chevy in for a 1942 Dodge ... the Dodge is a little better car than the Pontiac in that it has the Fluid Drive. This means that one can use the clutch to put the car in high and then never use the clutch or gear-shift again except to go backwards. When coming to a stop light one merely puts on the foot brakes to stop the car. To start forward the foot throttle is depressed to speed the motor up. The car moves slowly at first and then through the "Fluid Drive"catches up to the motor speed without any use of the clutch. Pretty tricky, eh? Must make a driver lazy. *(See page 120 for picture of Roger's Dodge.)* ¶ Thanks a lot for the dishes, Mom. They are very attractive and will serve us very well. There is nothing that you have to send us but I might as well list some of the things in case they are stored away at home: 2 large rugs, 2 throw down rugs, 1 bureau, 1 desk, 2 end tables, table liners. ¶ ... I guess all the family is back together for a while anyway. I do hope the long motor trip was successful and enjoyed by all. Am anxious to hear about it all.

Love to all, Rog

September 17, 1941. Grandpa to Roger (5 pages). Excerpts:
Forgive my negligence in not writing ... office more than busy with many complications ... Sunday: it was hot hot. Mother and I went for a long ride.. Enjoyed your last two letters so much dear son. They <u>are</u> such a comfort to Mother and to me & we appreciate so much your taking the time to write us often. ¶ Arrange for the car to be paid $100 per month for reasons that I gave. We are happy to send this to you dear son ... My calculations make it appear that you will be making $2,028 a year: is this correct? Not bad after two years.

September ? , 1941. Grandpa to Roger (6 pages).
Speaks about what he is doing to help support Roger: monthly check to help with expenses, monthly check for car payment, and provision of furniture, etc. for his apartment. He and Grandma:
... love to do for you. It gives us the greatest pleasure to do so. ... It is very comforting to Mother & I to know you have a comfortable home. One

cannot do good work if one doesn't. So many people fail in life because they are not intelligent enough that it is a <u>necessity</u>. Always watch it & never economize on food or comfortable habitation. Remember — rest, daily exercise outside — even if just a little, clean play, a little <u>good</u> reading every day, clean companions. <u>You</u> don't have to remember these things. With you they are second nature. Being a thoroughbred <u>you</u> require better care than a scrub — this you may need to <u>remember</u>. A good home, a good car, good clothing, good men require better care than cheap stuff — isn't it so? ¶ We appreciate so much what you said concerning our wonderful summer. It was indeed a happy one. Mother did more to make it happy than any one else. She worked <u>hard</u> all summer & was as always so wonderful in her understanding. She is more to be loved & thanked than I dear son. When you write next time tell her how grateful we are to her for her unselfish devotion too us all. There are few who would have been so self sacrificing. She did not have a holiday and rest from her labors as the rest of us did. Hence I want her to visit you a month this winter or early spring where she can loaf & do just what <u>she</u> wishes to do.

SEPTEMBER 28, 1941. GRANDPA TO ROGER (6 PAGES). EXCERPTS:
.. have been home a month..a tough month..morale of my office was zero and I have had to buck it up and this isn't easy. It is coming along. ¶ I am reading "Winged Warfare" by Gen H. H. Arnold Deputy Chief of Staff for air. Most illuminating and instructive as well as interesting. Upon completion will send to you for your library on air. Read! Read! Read! A new science and the man who reads and studies will go to the front. I will ask Gen Arnold — known as "Happy" in the service, to autograph it for you. ... ¶ Akin working hard. We have had no word from Sheldon yet. I hope and trust he will dig in. Mother is fine so we have much to be thankful for. ¶ I walk my 3.5 miles to office daily (via Rock Park) which keeps me fit. Mother and I ride twice a week. She rides almost daily in the early morning. Akin goes with us on Sunday. ... <u>Keep fit</u>. You will need it in business & maybe in the army. Keep fit mentally, physically, and morally & they <u>can't</u> hold you down, Such as you and I have to <u>work</u> for that. Others may not but mind that <u>we do</u>. ... ¶ Let us remember our plan of last year to have a talk once a month. It is now time.
ENCLOSED WAS A LETTER FROM HELEN TO GRANDPA. EXCERPTS:
.. I can't go to bed 'til I've told you again how very much the summer

with all of you meant to us and our wonderful, wonderful trip that will give us so much happiness all the rest of our lives. We are so grateful to you for making it all possible — and oh, dear ones, above all else I am grateful to you for making our marriage possible and giving us all these years of being together while Bill is in school. I love him so much and I'm so happy to be back in our little nook *(their apartment)* with all our things about us and again be making a home in which we both find so much happiness ... *Grandpa must have been supporting them while Bill in medical school.*

SEPTEMBER 28, 1941. ROGER TO GRANDPA. EXCERPTS:
San Francisco over the weekend, tennis Monday night, late nights working during the week, behind in his sleep, studying and correspondence.
... hope that I don't have too many weeks like that. Of course, my check will be a lot larger than usual, but I am not sure it is worth it. ¶ There is a very definite reason why we had to work so long this last week and that is that the Navy is concerned about the delivery of spare parts for its airplanes. Douglas is behind on its deliveries but apparently the need was so great that 'Washington' told Douglas something had to be done. All last week we were computing just what percentage of the spare parts had been delivered and just what delivery commitments in a percentage form could be made for the future. The whole picture gives me the impression that the Navy is attempting to acquire an excess of spare parts as a reserve for some contingency, and I am sure we all know what that is. I think it would be best to say nothing about this outside of the family as it might be of value to some outsiders.

OCTOBER 18, 1941. ROGER TO GRANDPA. EXCERPTS:
.. Navy and Army are getting ready to send a great many airplanes to the Philippines (significant ?) and the demand for spare parts has been heard and felt throughout the entire plant ... Even with all the service and maintenance parts supplied by Douglas, the navy has had a great deal of difficulty keeping its planes in service. At present there must be at least 10% of them grounded because of the need of some replacement part ... The thought of what might happen when war comes worries me if all of this trouble is experienced in peace time ... ¶ I hope everyone is well and happy at home. I never felt better even with the long hours ...

Rog

OCTOBER 27, 1941. GRANDPA TO ROGER. ENCLOSED IS A LETTER FROM SHELDON TO GRANDPA. EXCERPT:

... The Army has taken over Chapel Hill. About 4,000 come every weekend. They get drunk and tear up our Frat house and sleep in our beds. It is a mess. *Also enclosed is a letter from the owner of Camp Vonhurst in New Hampshire and a newspaper clipping announcing the retirement of General Hester, a friend of Grandpa's who had been helping with Roger's deferment. Gen Hester was relinquishing his command at Camp Wheeler and transferring to another camp. The article addressed "his deeply human side which endeared him" to all 18,000 men under his command. These were the sorts of men with whom Grandpa associated.*

OCTOBER 28, 1941. ROGER TO GRANDPA. EXCERPT:
He has just picked up his new Dodge Coupe (photo on following page).

I am very fortunate to have received delivery. After December 15 there will be no more chromium on automobiles and that will only be the beginning, other materials will be denied car manufacturers as this war develops.

NOVEMBER 17, 1941. ROGER TO GRANDPA. EXCERPTS:
His boss, Jim Farra, agreed to give Roger two days off at Christmas. He will fly American Airlines home for Christmas.

I am listening to the news on the radio and it seems that once again Russia is beating back the Germans. It has happened before and each time we thought that Germany's time had come but it turned out that the Nazis were only taking time to 'gird their loins' for a new thrust. Let's hope that this time will be different and that Russia will be able to inflict a stabilized war on Germany to give us more time. ¶ In six months the El Segundo Plant is scheduled to be turning out fifteen ships per week and the Long Beach Plant 80 ships per week. There are many new plants all over the country preparing to do the same. Of course all of these airplanes and other offense weapons are still on paper and the country is not equaling the production expansion made during equivalent time during the First World War. But it may be that we are planning to produce so very much more that the preparation and production of capital goods is of necessity taking more time. I really believe this is the case even though government red tape and restriction is anything but a contributing factor the speed.

Roger and his 1942 Dodge.

MONDAY, NOVEMBER 24, 1941. ROGER TO GRANDPA. EXCERPTS:

Sunday the weather was perfect, cool breeze, bright warm sun, and a brilliant blue sky without a trace of a cloud. Consequently, I wanted to take an airplane trip; so Geraldine Huber, a very nice girl from Montana who has been working at Douglas, and I flew to Palm Springs. At the altitude we flew it was very rough and gusty as there was a strong north wind blowing from the mountains, but once we arrived at Palm Springs everything was perfect. The people down there were roaming about in shorts, and I was inclined to do the same thing, except that I had no shorts, at least not the kind I could wear as my sole garment. ¶ It is exactly one month from now that I'll arrive in Washington. I can hardly believe it, but now that I am thinking about it the time seems to be passing slowly for the first time in many months. ¶ I have been following the record of Princeton's football team this year and it is terrible. The team has only won two games this whole year. Last Saturday Navy beat my 'alma mater' 23-0 and it cost me $4.00 in bets. I give up! Will see you soon, very soon.

Love to all, Rog

DECEMBER 1, 1941. ROGER TO GRANDPA. EXCERPTS:

I made my reservation on the American Airlines ... everything is all

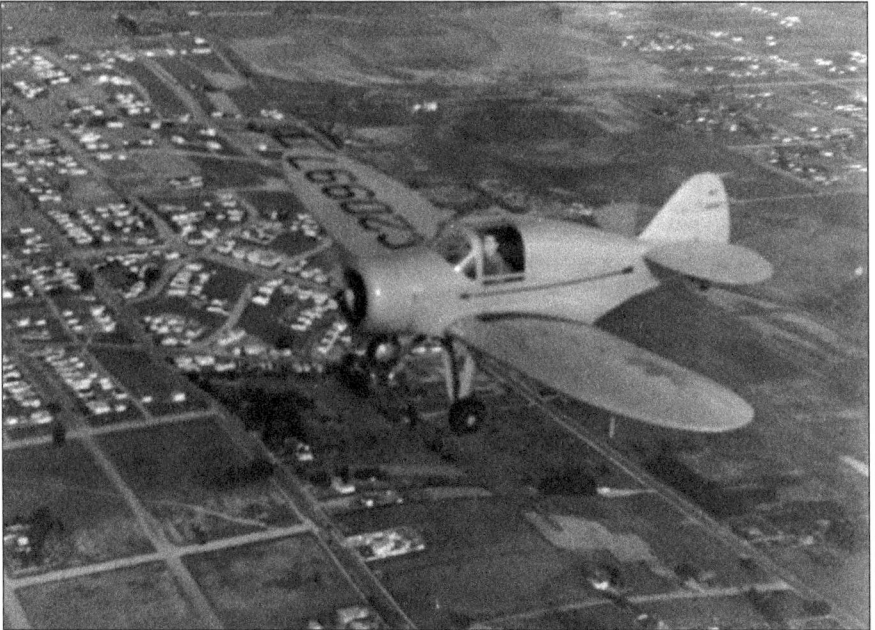

Roger's Culver Dart. Geraldine later said that she fell in love with Roger on their first date, when he took her for a ride in his plane.

set ... spent the whole weekend working on the Dart as it is now up for relicensing ... one thing about the ship that has been causing a lot of discussion between me and the mechanic. He claims that the main spar in the wing is split , and I claim that it is not ... from what I have learned at Douglas and from my experience with the ships around the airport I honestly don't believe the spar is split.. don't worry I am going to leave it on the ground until a competent inspector checks it, and that will be soon because I want to make that mechanic eat his words. ¶ .. one bit of news from the plant that is of special interest and that is that Douglas is building an attack bomber which carries a 75mm cannon in its nose (this is absolutely secret). Unless Germany is doing the same I feel sorry for her bombers. One shot from such an attack ship would correspond to a direct hit by an anti-aircraft projectile. ¶ For years I have been promising myself I would learn to ice skate and this year is no different, but I have a little added incentive. The girl from Montana, Gerry Huber whom I took to Palm Springs last week, is an excellent skater and has promised to hold me to my promise. So with a little pleasure thrown in with my work I may succeed this year.

SUNDAY, DECEMBER 7, 1941.

SURPRISE JAPANESE ATTACK ON PEARL HARBOR forces the U.S. into World War II. Vice-Admiral Chuici Nagumo led a 33-ship Japanese striking force that sailed under the cover of darkness to within 200 miles north of Oahu, third largest of the Hawaiian Islands. His carriers launched approximately 360 airplanes against the U.S. Pacific Fleet. The first bombs fell 7:55 A.M., Hawaiian Time. The primary targets were eight American battleships which were among the 92 naval vessels anchored in the harbor. The United States had 18 ships sunk or severely damaged, about 170 planes destroyed, and about 3,700 casualties. "Remember Pearl Harbor!" became the rallying cry for the United States in World War II. Two months later Roger and Geraldine Huber would be married.

DECEMBER 8, 1941. LETTER FROM ROGER TO GRANDPA. IN ITS ENTIRETY.

Dear Mom and Dad, This is one day we shall not forget for many a year. People are babbling everywhere expressing one opinion or another about something they know nothing of. All I know is that the trouble has started, only started, and I trust that we may act wisely and in a strong determined manner. ¶ The government has decreed that all private flying is to cease in this area so my Dart is now sentenced to a term in the hanger. I don't know how long it will be. I am sure that the restrictions will be relaxed somewhat in a very short time though because there are many students training at the Los Angeles Airport who will eventually find their way into the Army and Navy Air Corps and the government realizes this. I can't understand exactly why all private ships are grounded except that I have heard that the C. A. A. wants to check each and every pilot to check his citizenship status, etc. I have a feeling that in the end all student and pilot training will be allowed but that miscellaneous private flying for pleasure will be banned except in certain cases. Perhaps the fact that I am working for Douglas, am an officer in the reserve and am known in the Army through you, Dad, will enable me to continue flying. ¶ The Dart passed its relicensing examination with flying colors. After the checking by the mechanic only one minor adjustment had to be made. The most interesting part of the relicensing was that the mechanic had to swallow the statement he made indicating that the wing spar was cracked. ¶ Only 15 more days before I leave for home, and it still seems like a dream. I hope that the national defense for the area doesn't become so acute that pleasure flying is banned in the air lines. That would be too sad so I won't think any more about it. ¶ The rush for spare parts has already started. This morning we received a wire from the Bureau of Aeronautics requesting that we submit a list of <u>all</u> spare parts available and provide a revised delivery commitment for all spare parts on order. The shipment of spare parts to the Philippines I told you about nearly six weeks ago was significant as we understand only too well now. ¶ The suitcase I am bringing on the airplane doesn't carry much as you know. Will I need my tux, my tails or just a dark suit. You know what will be going on in Washington so let me know as no matter what suit I take I'll have to drag it out of the mothballs. ¶ The weather is still just perfect, warm bright sunny days, and crystal clear moonlight nights. But I do wish you could stir up a little snow for me around Christmas time. I would love to see it again on Lowell St.

Your loving son, Rog

DECEMBER 15, 1941. LETTER FROM ROGER TO GRANDPA. IN ITS ENTIRETY:
Grandpa wrote in his hand at the end of this letter:

One of the finest letters ever written by a <u>man</u>.
His father Xmas 1941

Dear Mom & Dad, I surely hate to write this letter because in it I have to say that I shall not be able to come home for Christmas. There are many reasons, but what makes it worst of all is that Jim Farra left it up to me whether he would try to push through my leave of absence. Many other boys and girls have had their Christmas trips home cancelled and if I should leave there would be hard feelings and a feeling of contempt for the Sales Department. Also, we are extremely busy now and every minute at the plant is important. In the future if things should suddenly go worse for us in the Pacific it would be essential that <u>every</u> Aircraft worker be at his post. I am no exception! And again the transportation facilities are overloaded and service for commercial passengers might be disrupted at any moment. In face of all these things, dear family, I just cannot bring myself to pull what strings I can in order to make the trip. At present we are working a six day week and as soon as the material becomes available I shall not be surprised to hear the announcement of a seven day week. ¶ Please tell what friends of mine you see at home that I truly did want to see them all this Christmas and feel very badly about not being home. ¶ The plant is now completely blacked-out. Every window is covered with black paint. As far as we in the office are concerned we might as well be on the third shift. But once in a while we do hear rumors that the sun is shining outside. Then we scamper out at lunch to see if it is true. The anti-aircraft defenses around the plants are improving rapidly. Guns, planes, concrete protection for aircraft, and barracks all appearing overnight. ¶ I tell you the above because I know you want to know what is going on. I am sure that the headlines back East are exaggerating every minor incident that is rumored out here. No one is panicky here, just mad like the rest of the country. We don't believe there is any danger present, but we are all glad that precautions are being taken <u>in case</u> danger should come. The first black-outs were a farce and every one became excited and started yelling at their neighbors to put the lights out. Even I yelled at the "damn" Jews next door who left everything wide-open. I think now though that a black-out would be nothing novel and no excitement would ensue. ¶ Truly folks, please don't worry, if you are at all, because most of us out here worry a little about the East Coast. I do believe some of these farmers are heading back to town.

My fondest love to each and every one of you, Rog

Christmas telegram to Davis family from Roger: Holiday Greeting by Western Union
THE DAVIS FAMILY= 3601 LOWELL ST NORTHWEST WASHDC=

SORRY I AM NOT WITH YOU AS WE PLANNED BUT AM WITH
YOU IN SPIRIT. MERRY CHRISTMAS TO YOU ALL= ROG

Forward from this point we have a limited number of Roger's letters.

*DECEMBER 26, 1941. ROGER TO FAMILY (LETTER SAVED BY VIVIAN). IN
ITS ENTIRETY.*

Dear family, Christmas day has passed once again and even though I
enjoyed it there wasn't a minute that passed that I didn't think of all of you
at home and wish that I could be there with you. However, what we have to
give up for this war is so little compared to what we are living and fighting
for that we should not mind it too much. ¶ I want to thank each and every
one of you for making my Christmas as happy as it could be away from
home. I didn't open any of your presents before Christmas but piled them
under our tree that Nora fixed so nicely. At 10:30 a.m. yesterday morning
I sat down and opened each one very carefully. I appreciated each one so
much and I thank you again from the bottom of my heart. George couldn't
enjoy his Christmas too much because he has had a bad cold and for the
last two days hasn't been able to say a word. I am only now becoming accustomed to having him speak in a whisper. ¶ Dad, I went over to the Santa
Monica Plant day before yesterday to do what I could about my military
matter. I believe Mr. Simpson, who writes letters for reserve officers for
Cover's signature, will write as good a letter as anyone could. However,
from what I learned talking to him it is only a matter of time before I
am called. Paragraph 2c of the bulletin No. 1 you sent me stated that the
War Department Reserve Pool would be kept, <u>but</u>, per paragraph 6 said
that these officers would also be called in order of priority. Another point
which has changed in the Pool is that in the list of information requested
about the officers there is a question concerning wages or salary. My base
rate is $39 per week so I am afraid that my importance will not seem very
outstanding in comparison with the need for expanding the Army. ¶ Nevertheless, Douglas will try its best to keep all officers. The respective letters
will all go forward at the same time, either this Saturday or next Monday
as all letters must be in the War Department by January 2, 1942. ¶ When
you send the .32 pistol and the camera, could you send my complete Army
uniform? I might as well have it let out so I can get my fat tummy into it. ¶
I know that my question about going into the Airs Corps is again coming

to the front. I still feel that any other branch of the service would be useless to me as far as my future life is concerned. However, I have no insane desire to become a pilot. As you said in your letter, Dad, I would probably do a great deal better in some administrative position. I heartily agree with you. What education and training I have had prepares me exactly for a position directly under the Supply Officers of some Army or Navy Depot. But does the Army know this? If you think it possible for me to do this I believe I should apply at once. I am not trying to avoid combat service because very often I grow angry and have a strong yearning to take my pilot training and be off, but I have many things to think of and will explain now. ¶ I had wanted to tell you this in a quiet family gathering around the fire yesterday at 3601 Lowell St. but since fate made it impossible I must resort to a letter. I was going to tell you that Geraldine Huber and I were very much in love with each other and wanted to be married. Our plan was to be sensible and wait until our families could be here next summer. But lately the complexion of the whole world has changed. The short time of waiting for anything and the time consumed in preparation and planning <u>was</u> nothing, but now all that seems to have changed. Six months seems a long time when at the end of that time there is a possibility that I might be on some foreign soil fighting a war of four, five or six years duration. Also, and I will never say this again dear family, there is the chance that I may never return. All of these things pass through my mind occasionally and seem to make me feel much older. The smaller interests of life I seem to have passed by. I look back, not forward to them. In view of all this Gerry and I want to be married very soon. I do not believe I am wrong in reasoning this way and I hope I have not been made hysterical by the war. Gerry and I have known each other for a year and have been together constantly since last September. *(Note: Roger's first mention of Geraldine was in his November 24, '41 letter when he took her on a trip in his airplane, about a month ago. Mom, Geraldine, told me often after Dad died that she fell in love with him on that first date in the airplane and that he asked her to marry him on their third date. Therefore, I believe that Roger, Dad, in order not to appear impetuous and alarm his parents, told them that they had been seeing each other for a longer period.)* Please advise me, Mom and Dad, and brothers and sister if you think I am wrong in this. It is very important to me. I don't feel upset or excited, but suddenly I feel that many years have been put behind me. ¶ I am sorry, oh, so sorry, that I had to write instead of saying this. It is so difficult to clarify one's feelings and attitude without personal contact but I hope I have been clear. ¶ Let me hear from you soon.

My fondest love to all of you, Rog

JANUARY 6, 1942. ROGER TO GRANDPA (LETTER SAVED BY VIVIAN). EX-CERPTS:

... I have been made so happy by the wonderful letters I have received from each member of the family during the past week. I felt sure all of you would understand about Gerry and me, but it just made me feel ever so much better to read it again and again. Each of you asked what she was like so I will try to tell you. Naturally I am prejudiced in her favor so you will have to take that into consideration. To describe her physically she is about 5' 4" tall, weighs 120 lbs. and is quite solid looking. *(See photo on following page.)* Her hair is a light brown and hangs down the back of her neck with small curls on either side of her head. Her eyes are a hazel color, I guess, because they are green, blue, brown and yellow all at the same time. And what makes her most like me is the fact that she has a round face and very even teeth. ¶ The people I have met since entering Princeton have been primarily of two types, one type always felt he was above every one socially and seem to have a false sense of values made up of sophisticated notions; the other type never seemed to have any sense of values or character even false. These made up the 'common herd' as we sometimes say. A few people fall in between these categories and Gerry is one of these. She comes from a rather small town, Glasgow, Montana. Her father is a ranch owner and school teacher and her ancestry is Swiss. She went to school in her home town until she finished high school and then went to Downer College for girls in Milwaukee for two years and then to the University of Montana for a year. At the end of that time she came here to California to visit her brother (Bob) who was working in the Timekeeping Department at Douglas with me. She decided to get a job at Douglas and has been here ever since. She has done very well at the plant since she has received several raises and now has quite a nice little posi-tion of responsibility *(Note: personal secretary to the President of Douglas Aircraft, Donald Wills Douglas, Sr.).* When she first started she had to take a course in Production Control. When the final exam was given Gerry took a mark higher than any of the boys who were working in the shop. ¶ All of these things I have told you only give you a history of what she has

Geraldine Emma Huber, born December 10, 1918. Written in Geraldine's hand on reverse:

Santa Monica, Calif
20 years old
I really didn't have much lipstick on.
They painted all pictures that dumb way!

done. As for the remainder of the description, I'll only try. Even though she works among the hard people of the world she is very sweet and gentle and very feminine. She loves pretty things and can't stand to have her apartment, which she shares with two other girls, in an untidy condition. I have never known her to have an unkind or an unsympathetic thought; and she has never been anything but honest with me and all of her friends, and of these she has a great many. ¶ And, above all, Mom and Dad, she wants a home of her own. Not a large one but one she can take care of. Her mother has been here ever since a few days before Christmas and apparently has taught Gerry the desire for and responsibilities of a home. I like Mrs. Huber very much as she is quite pleasant, generous, helpful to her children and very much a mother to them both out here. ¶ I feel I have done a poor job of this letter, so hurry Mom, I want you and Gerry to know each other very well.

Love to all, Rog

JANUARY 12, 1942. GRANDPA TO ROGER (8 LONG PAGES). EXCERPTS:
    Beloved son of mine, I have not thanked you for your thoughtful Christmas present. Those slippers are the pride & joy of my heart and I am much appreciative of your <u>time</u> and thought. You are ever the thoughtful and devoted son ... ¶ Mother is quite herself again and is looking forward with such deep joy in seeing you. Her love for you spans the universe my son. You are the pride and joy of her heart. No man ever in this world had a finer wife & no boys a more wonderful mother. All of (us) owe all we are to her loving care & thought. Friend, teacher, inspiration for all that is fine and good and noble. We are greatly blessed. ¶ Your letter was a joy and delight to us son. We thank you for your loving thought for us. Of course you know how eagerly we pondered each word. ¶ I am enclosing Helen's letter: She and Bill as are all of us, happy with Gerry & you in your happiness. I send my love to her by mother and by you and the wish to know & love her as my daughter. I know she is fine and true and loyal and will be the companion and partner in the love, trials and tribulations that but bind us closer and closer as the years pass. May our dear Lord guide and watch over you both in the years to come. Nothing can matter much as long as a man can have the loyalty and care of a good woman, God's greatest gift. ... I shall be there whenever it *(their wedding)* takes place my son to give you my dearest blessing ... Dear boy guard your health & strength. Get sufficient

rest. 8 hours sleep is not enough. 10 hours is required. Get it. It will repay you in handsome dividends. Do not exhaust yourself because you have the reserve <u>now</u>. Keep that reserve as long as you can. You will need it. Try for a little out of doors each day though it is only a few minutes. A few times around the block taking great deep breaths. It is remarkable what 10–15 minutes daily of that will do. ... Dear boy your description of Gerry, her previous life and what she has done is very wonderful and makes us feel she is a fine little girl & that we love her. What you said about her mother and her love for and rearing of her children gives us confidence and joy. If Gerry has the home instinct then she is a real <u>woman</u>. <u>That</u> is what a <u>man</u> wants. The <u>home</u> instinct. It spells happiness, contentment and strength and may you two have all of that, and you will. ..She is the girl of your choice and we are <u>all</u> prepared to take her into our hearts and our lives. All the world loves lovers & we are foremost in that. As a family we are closely knit as you so well know. It is the inheritance of the Scots, particularly the Highland *(mountain)* Scots. Love me love my family: love my family and we love you. The contrary is also true. Offend my family & you offend me. I think I have instilled this into your personality unconsciously. Closely knit families make for a brave & courageous nation that can never be broken down. To love deeply; to be devoted to the family and the home is the heritage of a fighting conquering (with consideration) nation. Of that blood we come and I am sure does Gerry. May the blessing of God rest upon you and upon her for ever. It is the prayer of an old soldier the veteran of some wars. Would that if I were young again to give something more to my country. Our family has not lacked in this since the earliest days of the Republic. The military history while not brilliant is of service well & honorably done. Of this as a family we have a right to be proud. ... All things will work out for the best my beloved son. Here is home & love for you & your family as long as Mother and I live. In <u>our</u> hearts are enshrined the faces and the hearts of our beloved sons & their loved ones & so shall it be until we cross the Great Divide.

God bless & keep you beloved son of my heart. Dad

FEBRUARY 4, 1942
Roger and Geraldine Huber are married at St. Alban's parish in Westwood Village, Los Angeles (on the UCLA campus). Grandpa was best man. Renée and Gerry's parents were there. Roger was 25 years old, Geraldine 24.

Roger and Geraldine on their honeymoon in Rancho Santa Fe (north of San Diego).

FEBRUARY 12, 1942. ROGER TO GRANDPA (LETTER SAVED BY VIVIAN). IN
ITS ENTIRETY.

Dear Mom & Dad, Gerry and I have been married eight days now and we can hardly believe it. It really is difficult to realize, but we are both ever so happy that we did take that. I know that as far as I am concerned every passing day makes me love and admire her more. I know that she is the right girl for me and that she will do her duty beside me through good times and bad. ¶ When we arrived back here Sunday evening we found your thoughtful little notes and telegram and were so happy to have them. The four days at Rancho Santa Fe were very enjoyable as the weather was perfect and there were few people. *(See photos above.)* Also the visit with the Boones on Saturday was very enjoyable, but we were glad to return to our home even though the painters had not quite finished and the apartment was not

Roger and Gerry arrive at their first apartment, at 633 9th Street, Santa Monica, California.

put back together very well. If it hadn't been for Mrs. Huber's and Nora's working Sunday morning nothing would have been ready. But they hurried the painters and then did a great deal of work themselves. We are most grateful to them. ¶ Monday and Tuesday evenings we ate dinner downstairs as the kitchen was full of paint, and then spent the rest of the evenings arranging clothes, closets, pictures, etc. Wednesday was the first real homey evening we had and tonight the second. I believe Nora is very pleased that she is taking care of us so our home is working out wonderfully well. ¶ Mom, I received your letter today and everything listed there against what we had here in the apartment. Everything was present. Thanks so much for those other gifts you gave us. The bedside table, chair, etc. All add greatly to our bedroom. And I don't know how to thank both of you, Mom and Dad, for all the wonderful things you did for Gerry and me. It was perfect to have you both here and even though our wedding should have overshadowed everything else, it couldn't detract one little bit from the joy of the three of us being together. ¶ I am sorry to hear that I am no longer in the Pool, but of course we knew it would come sooner or later. And now that everything has broken loose I do hope the Air Corps Material Division will accept me. I could learn so much there and I feel that I could do them a great deal of good in a very small way. However, if the War Department sees fit to leave me in the Field Artillery I'll be only to glad to give what I can to protect our country, and from the looks of things now it appears that we all will have to start giving a lot more than we already have in order to save ourselves from disaster. If I should be called to active duty in the F. A. *(Field Artillery)* I would undoubtedly be sent to a rather out of the way post where wives could not very well go because my military record states that I am single.

Do you think it would be advisable to notify the Army of my change in status so that for the next year or two anyway before an A.E.F. *(American Expeditionary Forces)* Gerry and I might have some chance of being together? ¶ Every evening when I come home I hope to find good news about the Air Corps so I'll keep my fingers crossed. ¶ Gerry and I thank you again from the bottom of our hearts for the wonderful way you treated and received us. You are the best Mom & Dad a boy ever had.

Love to all at home, Rog

FEBRUARY 21, 1942. ROGER TO GRANDPA. EXCERPTS:

At first it seemed very strange to come home to a wife. I just couldn't believe it, but now I understand it very well. Every day I understand it better and love it more. Gerry and I are so very happy and grow happier every day, ... ¶ .. work at the plant..not as busy as one might believe. After the first jolt at Pearl Harbor the immediate demand for rush spare orders has decreased to the pre-war proportion. I don't know why it is but it might be that the ships which were smashed at Hawaii have been torn down even further and that the remains are furnishing the spare parts. This is what England has been doing for a long time. ¶ *Roger questioning again whether this a good time to leave Douglas if he could get what he wants in the Air Corps — his advance at Douglas temporarily blocked because of his pending Army draft status.* I have no wish at all to leave except to go where I can be of equal or better service to the country ... I don't blame Douglas one little bit if they are preparing themselves for the future <u>but</u> so am I. ¶ ... Gerry, Bob *(Gerry's brother who works at Douglas and who had introduced his sister to Roger)*, Mrs. Huber and I took a nice long drive (very slowly though in order to save the tires) up the coast and back through a long canyon which leads into San Francisco Valley. Then to my airplane to see if it was OK and so home. *(See following page for pictures taken on this drive.)*

MARCH 1, 1942. GRANDPA TO ROGER (10 LONG PAGES). EXCERPTS:

Dearest Daughter & Son, ... When American boys get to shooting they are really having themselves a time as the Rats (Japs) are due to learn later. MacArthur (please note he is a Scot 'even as you & I', Rog) Give that man an army & equip it, supply it & he will shoot the pants, if any, off the Rats. He is a genius and like all such is queer and not too popular among his fellow officers. I have known him for years and I assure you that he has the most alert

TOP: *Melinda Baechler Huber, Gerry's mom. ABOVE: Gerry's brother Bob and his fiancé, Eleanor. Bob had introduced Gerry to Roger.*

& brilliant mind I have ever come in contact with. It scintillates, flashes & boosts its brilliance that is dazzling. He sees a difficult problem, a pause a moment of intense concentration and the gist of the matter is his. Like such minds he is unstable but as a brilliant fighter my opinion is that the world at this time holds not his equal. Some day I would be glad to tell you some incidents concerning him. ¶ *Again Grandpa working his contacts in the Army for Roger. Be patient. A sensitive and confusing time ...* give not one word of this to **anyone**, not even a hint, not an allusion. You keep quiet & do all the listening. It is wonderful what you can learn by so doing. Dear mother taught me that. ... The real reason behind all of this *(confusion)* is an era making reconditioning (they call it reorganization) of the whole military establishment. It is entirely archaic as you know, Rog. Arnold *(a good friend of Grandpa's)* is the chief moving spirit & he is battling for his official life & the lives of millions of our youth. I wish we could discuss this. It will result in a new army organized for fighting which our army has never been! It has always been ordered on a peace basis, but the army is a war machine. ¶ Keep us informed of any happenings there; little incidents may be of value. ¶ You may remember beloved son while you were at Princeton I told you the Heroic age would come in your life, when our country would lead & the flag would fly from the Arctic Circle to Tierra del Fuego. It is here! We shall win: we have the spirit, the power, the intelligence to overcome the powers of darkness. We shall fight another Armageddon & we shall win & I know my sons will distinguish themselves. It is in the blood. Since the days of Killiecrankie & far back of that, since George Rogers Clark, the Civil War we have ever played a many part. Your Dad has seen service in 5 wars. Spanish American, Philippine Insurrection, Moro campaigns, Mexican War of 1916 (not 1847!) & the

World War. I have no decorations but an honorable record of excellent service in combat & elsewhere. ¶ Your letter expresses dear son what I would expect you to say. It gives your mother and I deep satisfaction & enlarges & deepens our love & esteem & respect for you — if such were possible. May our dear Lord abide with you my children. Your characters will be able & ready to withstand the shock of war & duty & the satisfaction & serene peace that shall follow will be deep & lasting. ¶ Here is home for those our sons may have to temporarily leave behind. This is home that darling Mother and I have denied ourselves to make and keep for you, your wives, your children. There is room and a warm & loving welcome always. To have those we love beneath this roof is the supreme pleasure & joy of life. Son if & when you are ordered to duty Gerry's home is here if she desires it. We will love & cherish her & her children for you until your return. Such extremity may not be, yet I must say this because a man must know his loved ones are safe & in the love of his family if he has a heart for his duty wherever it may lay. So Gerry is here when she wants & requires it so long as Mother and I may live. And believe me we are going to be about for a long time. Scots are tough & long lived. Dr. Graham was 101 plus when he passed over the Great Divide. Hence I figure I have about 35 years!! ¶ Mother and I think that what you describe in your last letter as having happened regarding orders in the plant as follows: They know as an officer of the Reserves you <u>will</u> be called to the colors. Hence business acumen & selfishness requires that they train a man whom the local draft board will be likely to defer as long as they can. This they are doing. It is not because you are less efficient & highly thought of but because they are looking to their own interests. This is the rule of life. Look you also to your interests with regard to your future. Possibly your future, aye more than possibly — probably will be greatly augmented by your experience with the army. In my opinion it will. The greater experience; the deeper knowledge brought about by your military career possibly as mine was from the Arctic Circle to the Equator will be of inestimable value to you. The boys who hugged the fireside will be minor appoints. You will be in the major circle where men of courage, experience, brains and <u>physical</u> superiority will be in control. Consider Pershing, Harbord, Andrews, Fox Conner (see your military history which you did <u>not</u> have at Princeton). Note your history of the Civil War. The leaders of the South & of the North controlled this country until they all passed on of age. Read the lives of Lee, Sherman, Grant, Sam Houston, etc. The leaders have been military men, the followers have been reptilian professional politicians. Ponder this my son and my daughter — nothing ventured, nothing gained. To the conqueror belong the spoils. To the Biblical accounts of the Talents. History is replete with it. ¶ May an old soldier say just that 10 minutes reading of the Bible will be oh so well worthwhile. Just 10 minutes every day. As you know son I am not deeply religious. I am not a constant churchman but the Bible has it all — the past, present & the <u>future</u> — the greatest book ever written. The 10 Commandments the greatest set of rules ever envisioned. Experience of a long life teaches me this is true. ¶ Right you are son to prepare yourself for the future as does Douglas ... About your service in the Army. Be prepared for lack of coordination, for frustration, for stupidity. 'Tis the way of democracy but it gives individualism where <u>perfect</u> military discipline allows no such opportunity. Exercise patience, do what you are told. Keep your mouth ***<u>shut</u>***. Button your lips & unbutton your eyes & ears. Write a journal by the day & send it to me for your future. You have no idea of what it will be worth. Overlook: rise above & see with the eyes of the eagle & not with the eyes of the mole (who has none). Read; read; read & read again. Military history. <u>Study your job</u> which consists in doing the daily stint but read! Read!! Read!!!! Your job for the moment be military. Fit yourself for it by study: by being physically, mentally & morally fit. The temptations will be <u>ever</u> present, day & night & particularly for such a comely youth as you are. ***<u>Do not yield.</u>*** The mental, physical & moral discipline thus engendered will make you ***<u>strong</u>***. All this have I been through. My companions who yielded have been gone these thirty years. Cashiered; died in brawls; suicide or simply disappeared; 'went native'; became beach combers; deserted the army & so were lost. Those of us who survived have more or less distinguished ourselves in military or civil life. The going was hard when we did not join the drinking, gambling and lady (natives) parties. It was lonely but good books & an eye to the future quickly cured that. ¶ I have advised you to touch no liquor in the military service. A glass of beer so as not to be considered straight laced. A quiet exit & bright & clear eyed on the job the next day. It payed me handsome dividends ... ¶ Sheldon registered & returned to college. By gosh he *is* a man; you said it right. Poor chap has a bad handicap but his ***<u>will</u>*** & his fine physique & superior intelligence will overcome it. I refer to his eyes & his allergic state. ¶ All is quiet, well ordered & happy at home. <u>Now</u> you & Gerry know what home is & why I love it so. 'Tis God sent & wife makes it so. May God bless <u>our</u> home: yours & mine — ours. Our home is given to you when it is so ordained that you may come to it.

(A personal note from me, Robert Davis, February 21, 2016: One of the most beautiful and inspiring letters I have ever read! I cry every time I read it.)

MARCH 8, 1942. GRANDPA TO ROGER (5 LONG PAGES). EXCERPTS:

Beloved 'children' ... Conserve your auto tires as well as those of your plane. Lock your car always & <u>watch your tires</u>. They are stealing them by the thousands and they never get them back. <u>Keep this in mind</u> ...

All happiness to you in these Halcyon days.

MARCH 10, 1942.

Just over a month after getting married Roger receives letter calling him to active duty effective March 14, 1942. To proceed "without delay" to Fort Mason, California to report to the Commanding General, San Francisco, Port of Embarkation for duty with the 399th Quartermaster Port Battalion (HQ 1st Military Area — Presidio of San Francisco).

Roger wanted to be in the Air Force (called the Army Air Corps at that time, name later changed to the Army Air Forces and eventually an independent department of the Department of Defense called the Air Force). He called Grandpa, who called his close personal friend, General Hap Arnold (commanding general of the Army Air Corps). The Army Air Corps comprised all of our air forces at that time. "Hap" had Roger's orders changed to Wright Field, Ohio, as a 2nd Lieutenant in the Army Air Corps with the Air Corps Material Division.

MARCH 13, 1942. GRANDPA TO ROGER (AND HENCEFORTH ALSO TO GERRY) EXCERPT:

Hurriedly written 2 pages.

... You're going to a wonderful station and will enjoy it. Now watch your time. I advise you both to drop your jobs and get your things packed and get off at once. Don't tarry. You belong to a different era now. You are entering a new life and you should look forward not backward.

MARCH 14, 1942.

Fort Mason Army Field Artillery orders revoked. Roger now ordered to proceed to Wright Field, Dayton, Ohio to report to Commanding Officer, Material Division.

MARCH 24, 1942. DART CRASHES.

Roger had put his Culver Dart airplane up for sale in Santa Monica at a price of $1,700. When Roger moved to Wright Field he arranged for a friend to fly his plane to him in Ohio. Shortly into his flight to Roger the pilot crashed the Dart in the mountains approximately 80 miles east of Santa Monica (in Mill Creek Canyon near Fallsville, California). The pilot suffered a broken back. Per the investigative report the pilot claimed that "lack of power output necessitated a forced landing in the river bed." The investigation disclosed "no evidence of structural or mechanical failure" and the probable cause of the accident was "Action of pilot in attempting to fly at low altitude, over rapidly rising terrain, in a low-powered aircraft" (mountains in the vicinity were covered by clouds). Though damaged, the plane was still in good enough condition to be salvaged but without Roger's knowledge rescuers carried the plane down the mountain. It was too heavy for them to bring down in one piece so they cut the wing assembly into two pieces. But a unique feature of the "Dart" was its "very wide, elliptical cantilever wing utilizing the low-aspect ratio concept that its designer wanted. This design, coupled with the wing's laminated spruce spar beams, resulted in the Dart having exceptional strength, rigidity and neck-jerking maneuverability." What this meant was that the two wings were part of one strong beam, and once cut rendered the aircraft useless. Dad had owned his plane for two and a half years, had received immeasurable joy from it, and had used it, along with his personal charm, to woo Geraldine to marry him.

MARCH 26, 1942.

Roger's "Date of Entry on Active Duty" into the U.S. Army. At Wright Field he went through 3 different titles on the same job while the Dept. of Defense was going through a period of reorganizing. Wright-Patterson Air Force Fields were divided into two Commands: the Material Command at Wright Field under General Bradshaw and the Air Service Command at Patterson Field. Dad worked for Colonel Turner Sims (nicknamed "Admiral" Sims while he was a 2nd Lieutenant at West Point. There was a well-known Admiral in the Navy at that time named Admiral Sims so he assumed that nickname. He was called 'Admiral' by his friends until the day he died). In the beginning Roger's primary job was liaison with the Air Service Command at Patterson.

APRIL 20, 1942. GRANDMA TO ROGER. EXCERPT:

... Sunday the Boones arrived at 5:15 and at 5:30 the Tea guests began to arrive — about 40 in all — just very old friends of the Boones — Chief Justice and Mrs. Stone came. (*Chief Justice Harlan F. Stone was the 12th Chief Justice of the U.S.. Joel and Helen Boone were two of Grandpa & Grandma's closest friends.*)

APRIL 24, 1942 - ROGER TO GRANDPA. EXCERPTS:
This is the first of the last 3 letters we have from Roger to Grandpa. Roger & Gerry living at 200 Park Road, Dayton, Ohio.

It has been quite a while since I have written you personally but every time I ask Gerry 'have you told the family about ---?' she says she has just written you about it. ... I have never had so little <u>real</u> work to do (because Gerry does it all) and yet had so little free time. *Roger explains the functions of the office where he works* — I could not be in a more advantageous position for learning the organization of the Army Air Force (AAF), the 'Air Corps' doesn't exist anymore. I have been working in the same room with Col. Sims, called 'Admiral' because he is a distant relative of the old Admiral Sims..Peculiar, though, ..he has a heart of gold. He has made arrangements to have me shown through almost every section at the Field — Contract, Production Engineering, Experimental Engineering, etc. I don't think very many people have ever been given that opportunity, and I surely do appreciate it. ¶ Every day I realize how fortunate I am to have such a wonderful wife. She is such a sane girl and such a hard worker. Our room is the cleanest and prettiest room in the house with flowers in it, etc.

MAY 24, 1942. GRANDPA TO ROGER (AND TO GERRY AS ALWAYS). 4 LONG PAGES. EXCERPT END OF LETTER,
..Your letters dear girl are a great joy & comfort to us and we appreciate very deeply your giving of us your time to do it. It means a great deal to us. Just now particularly because we know how absorbing your life is; newly married, a new life, so much of interest, so much to learn. You are <u>a darling</u> & our boy is indeed fortunate in you.

Fondest love to our 'children' from your ever loving Dad

MAY 31, 1942. GRANDPA TO ROGER (5 LONG PAGES). EXCERPTS:
(*If questions arise concerning Wright Field status*) ... Gen Arnold, Col. York, etc. could assist. It is not wise to use such influence too much. This you will understand without further comment. My desire & dear Mother's

is always to do for our children what may be best for their present & future welfare. For this we live. Your & Gerry's welfare is our <u>greatest</u> concern ... <u>Take your time</u> in advancing to flying status ... *(keep me advised)* Give us time & we can do a lot. Such things have to be done with much finesse. The situation is confused & no one may say what may happen.. *(Gerry)* is a Queen at waiting bless her darling heart. Aren't we fortunate to have such a daughter & you such a wife. ¶ *(Grandpa has advised Roger about his uniforms in many past letters)* Get good quality that looks nice & soldierly. You can afford it — do afford it. It will take you places. Dress nicely both of you & put on a front. It helps a lot in the Army ... Be snappy; stand up; keep your shoulders back & your tummy in & stand on your feet & look a man right in the eye. Salute with a snap. Move with a snap. Alert, decisive and quick. That's the Regular Army & it means <u>a lot</u>.

June 7, 1942. Grandpa to Roger (7 long pages). Excerpts:

(Akin has graduated from St. Albans) Akin's final marks are outstanding ... could go to any college he wished ... I think Princeton is the place. Rog, what do you think? If you have time to write him a short note congratulating him & encouraging him for Princeton it would please & encourage him immensely. He thinks you hung the moon in the sky son. He is a most affectionate and loyal soul & recognition of these virtues by you means a great deal to him. *(Bill will graduate from medical school March 1943 and the War Dept. allows him a year of training before he is called to active service — he has accepted internship at Wilmer Ophthalmology Institute, part of Johns Hopkins Hospital in Baltimore.)* So now I am exceedingly happy about my three boys. What it means to see you going onward & upward in life you will fully understand when your children grow to that age. It will be to you as it is to me the deepest satisfaction of your lives. ¶ Sheldon is having his troubles; but he will come along in time. He is a grand boy & has many high qualities. Study is as yet his bête noire; he will overcome this. ... Akin has elected to remain at home & study & read all the forenoons. He wants to study his music (piano) some; Mother will give him an art course at the National Gallery (the Mellon Gallery). He will probably take a course in typing. The lad has developed into a splendid young man. Handsome, intelligent & with a thorough & cleancut idea in what to do. Quiet & ever suave but with plenty of what it takes. ... Gerry, you will find as your experience grows that our Rog is most versatile. He can do anything & well. We

join you in being proud of him ... What you say about him being interested with important work is indeed significant. We appreciate you writing that Gerry. You are a jewel dear daughter to us & to Rog.

JUNE 21, 1942. GRANDPA TO ROGER (6 LONG PAGES). EXCERPTS:
(Roger's situation not likely to be changed.) ... Wright Field is the darling of the Air Force & I am sure they will not disturb its equilibrium to obtain a mere pilot. Of course I may be wrong ... ¶ Col. Hargreaves is leaving the air office here for Patterson Field. He is of the Medical Corps & I think very well informed in air matters. One of my lecturers in the Post Graduate Course on several occasions..would be proper (and good judgement) if you & Gerry called upon them. He knows of you & would be a nice contact for you. ... remember to take off time to observe the amenities of military life. Not many of your friends know them. You have a great advantage in knowing them ... ¶ I imagine Rog gets a lot out of the Reserve Officers meetings. Watch his rest Gerry: <u>fatigue is cumulative</u>. Put down in figures. He should have at a minimum 9 hours of sleep. Figure out at the end of each week how many hours he is short & you will see how much fatigue he has in the red side of the account. Multiply that by 4.5 & you get the monthly liability. Keeping that up means lessoning of energy; failing efficiency & reduction of the <u>quality</u> of his cerebration. That means a lessoning of his efficiency. That was in no small part the cause of the Pearl Harbor humility & ghastly defeat!! Ponder this very soberly my children. Social life in the Army is nice & should be indulged in <u>but</u> not where it interferes with the main issue. Forgive me if I weary or offend you. It is only my great love for you and concern for your future. I have lived in the Army. I have seen many fine officers & many fine women go on the rocks with too much social life. Don't let it get into your blood. It is incidental as it was in college!! Keep your <u>feet on the ground</u>.

JUNE 28, 1942. GRANDPA TO ROGER (7 LONG PAGES). EXCERPTS:
... Tell us the time Sunday for the conference telephone call. I will try then to arrange with Helen, Bill & Sheldon so we can have a nice visit every two weeks. Please children don't forget to tell me the time best suited for you. It means much to the 'Old Folks at Home' ... ¶ The war doesn't seem encouraging does it? Our allies English & Chinese seem to be on their knees (or tummies). France is under the axe. But we will win because we have to.

That is a study in psychology for you two. When we <u>have</u> to do it, we do it! 'Tis in the anglo saxon scotch german etc. etc. Americans to do the job & we <u>will</u>. Would to almighty God I was again going to make five us. But I am doing my bit — quite a bite. The doctors are on the preferred list son, in the Service & in civilian life. I am doing 12-15 hrs. a day and at 66 that isn't too bad.. ¶ .. I think what you heard of returning the officers to their different Corps was a repercussion of the hangers on in Washington. There are thousands of them here. Some (possibly many) political favorites & the country grows restive under this situation. As much as we would love to have Gerry & you here we are glad for your sake son that you are not. ¶ How about the yellow fever inoculations, many have been made ill & some have died as a result of it. I softened it for you; tell me of it. This is more important than you know. Keep your mouths shut & your eyes and ears <u>very</u> wide open <u>and</u> advise the old Dad. Being an old soldier, the veteran of 3 wars & several 'Banana Wars' (army slang for the wars in Mexico, Panama & Central America etc. etc) my experience may be of use to you — if you keep in touch with me. ¶ The Carabao — Military Order of the Carabao — will shortly elect me Grand Wheel & Lead — meaning Secretary & Treasurer. They wanted to make me Paramount Carabao but I declined. I think that belongs to the Fighten' Man. Medical Officers are non combatants under the Geneva Convention (Gerry go to the library & look this up, it will be of value to Rog & you) <u>but</u> when you are fighting Barbarians all civilized rules are off. That was where my fighting was & so it is now. Gerry get Lamb's *Life of Genghis Khan*. Read it <u>now</u> & get Rog to read it. Enjoy your friends my beloved children but do some solid reading else your brains grow dull. Remember Pearl Harbor! Too much social chit chat, lack of contemplation & study, lack of bodily vigor as a result of too much social chit chat, drinks, alleged food etc etc & all that goes with it. It destroyed Rome, the Venetian Republic, England. Read Plato's <u>Republic</u> ***not*** Democracy. Don't be led astray by the Army social life. Use it; don't let it <u>use you</u>. ¶ Forgive me if I seem to preach; 15 years in the Army taught me much. I would pass this experience on to my daughters & my sons. Gerry don't let the Army teach you to drink. Remember those who are to be the next generation. <u>They</u> cannot be strong if you are not!! See Mendel & his laws. MENDEL. Children of mine use your good brains, the education & the character that your father & mother Gerry & <u>your</u> father & mother Rog have given you at <u>great sacrifice</u>. Don't fall into dissolute habits, hours or doings. It <u>spells ruin</u>, unhappiness & worse than death. Stand firm, stand resolute. Because 'they' do thus & <u>so you</u> don't have to do so. Let the conscience that both inherited & had by environment & in your home guide you. And may our Dear Lord ever keep watch over is our constant prayer. Pray do not let me offend you; 'tis only my <u>great</u> love that prompts me to so write.

Devotedly, Dad

JUNE 29, 1942 -ROGER TO GRANDPA. EXCERPTS:
Roger and Geraldine living at 2226 Emerson Avenue, Dayton, Ohio. This is the second of the last three letters we have from Roger to Grandpa.

... Saturday after work Gerry and I drove to Fort Thomas, KY to spend the weekend with Lt. & Mrs. B. J. Woods. He is in the Medical Corps and she is Gerry's best friend. *(Vonnie Woods remained Gerry's best friend for life.)* They really are fine people, a lot of fun, well raised and plenty of good sense. They took very good care of us. That night we went to the Post dance, and Sunday we saw really good tennis matches ... ¶ It was a relief to receive the insurance money for the Dart.. A friend of mine out there..said that the front of the ship was terribly damaged in the accident and that all the rest of the damage was done later. The 'farmers' who moved the plane chopped off the wings instead of removing the bolts. Also, the instruments, tires, etc. were all stolen by people who visited the accident. ¶ The raise that Congress just gave the Army surely is going to come in handy here. What I get now under the new set up is: $150 base pay, $7.50 longevity pay, $65 rent, $42 subsistence. $264.50 total. About $7.00 a month goes to life insurance and $18.50 for War Bonds, but even at that we can't complain.

JULY 5, 1942. GRANDPA TO ROGER (4 LONG PAGES). EXCERPTS:
Continues to offer him contacts.

... Do you get an emotion in going to KY ? The state which our forebears help form & build & furnishing the men who conquered from the British that great territory north of the Ohio. We had <u>two</u> ancestors on that expedition of 174 men son. It is something one may rightly be proud of ... ¶ Sheldon..is deeply and sincerely desirous of getting into the service ... ¶ What a shame that ghouls so treated your beloved Dart. Our lower classes to which the politicians appeal are awful — 'po white trash' the very scum of the earth. ¶ *(Concerning Roger's raise:)* .. Why the $18.75 for War Bonds? Is that required & by whose authority? ..

July 10, 1942.
Roger promoted to 1st Lieutenant, U.S. Army.

July 12, 1942. Grandpa to Roger (as always also to Gerry). 4 long pages. Excerpts:

Congratulations dear children ... Gerry darling I know how happy you. How it takes Mother and I back 25 years ago last March when Roger arrived at 4 A.M. on a beautiful Spring morning. Your baby will arrive about March too & won't we be happy ... You are young & so strong & athletic. Such women have no trouble & neither will you; God Bless you dear daughter ... *(Grandpa gives them comprehensive advice on obtaining & working with the best obstetrician & hospital)* Remember I am a Doctor and of course you know no one could be more interested than I. ¶ ... I am sure your commission as 1st Lieutenant will be along shortly but don't be worried if it doesn't; red tape is very time consuming. It wouldn't surprise me if you are a Captain by the time you are a Daddy! ¶ Gerry dear your letter of June 30 was so enjoyable. You write such nice newsy letters which we enjoy & appreciate so much. ..You are a darling daughter to us & we love you devotedly. *Enclosed is letter from Akin. Excerpt:* Dad and Mother have just told me the great news. So you are going to be parents and I am going to be an uncle! It doesn't seem possible. Congratulations.

July 28, 1942. Grandpa to Roger (3 long pages) Excerpts:
Thanks Gerry for her letter.

We will go to Vonhurst Outer Harbor next week. Mother & Akin, Bill & Helen & later myself. Sheldon's military matters keep me here a bit longer. ¶ Son spare no necessary expense in taking care of daughter from now on. I shall back you fully so do not worry about finances. What is money but to do for those we love.

August 2, 1942. Grandpa to Roger (and as always Gerry). 4 long pages. Excerpts:

.. We understand perfectly darling why you cannot come to us in New Hampshire & we love you all the more if such could be, for staying on the job. It is what we thought you would do & we admire your devotion to Rog & to your duties. It spells happiness in the future for you both ... ¶ Will you children do something for me? Go to the best photographer in town and have some of the best photos taken of each of you, and one together and have the man send the bill to me. The last I <u>insist upon</u>. Please don't argue now on this my first request since your wedding day. Rog to have on his new uniform. Don't we wish we were all at Palos Verdes for August!! Keep quiet about the photos because I want us to surprise Mother. I want you to order as many as you wish. Gerry will want to send some to her folks & friends & you too. ..I want one of the two of you for my office. *(See photos on following pages.)* ¶ Rog, I am eye examiner for the Cargo plane* set up that you have no doubt heard of. It is staggering to the imagination. They plan to have a big ship out of the Wash. airport for overseas every 15 minutes & one landing every 15 min,!!.. ¶ If the opportunity comes keep me informed on the possibility of transferring to the Air Forces. You have a good & legitimate reason for so doing ... I am sure General Arnold would do anything he could ...

AUGUST 10, 1942. GRANDPA TO ROGER (5 LONG PAGES). EXCERPTS:
Family has arrived at Vonhurst Outer Harbor in N. H.

.. Rog, I don't wish to load any of my responsibilities on you but you can advise & possibly help me in Sheldon's matters. Poor boy his semi-invalidism in his early youth & adolescence so interfered with his work & school that he got no foundation and did not learn to study or how to study. In consequence he has done poorly at UNC. His draft number will be called at the end of August. He may be refused on account of has asthma and myopia. There <u>are</u> places in the service for those somewhat handicapped. While Sheldon is not a good student, he is alert and smart & wants to get into the service with all his heart. He is deeply interested in the service and would do well in it. He has had 2 yrs. in Junior Military Academy *(Riverside Academy)*. Do not ask anything of anybody but only information and advice. ... ¶ The officers I know who are in a position to know feel that if the Russian army isn't destroyed by winter that Hitler's chances for success are bad. They feel that the loss of territory is bad but not fatal but the loss of the Army would be fatal. ¶ Gerry are you feeling

---

Grandpa enclosed a newspaper article titled "Freight Trains of the Air." "... Can a flying ship be built that will carry 80 tons of cargo to Europe at a speed of 300 miles an hour? Will big transports tow half a dozen gliders, each with several tons of freight; actually freight trains of the air?" See American Airpower Comes of Age: General Henry H. "Hap" Arnold's World War II Diaries.

Roger and Geraldine (one month before Rogie was born). Grandpa had insisted that they use the best photographer in their area and then send him the bill.

This was another picture requested by Grandpa and was Gerry's favorite photo of Roger. After Roger's death in 2004, she kept a 3x4" framed copy on her nightstand and kissed it every night before she fell asleep. It remained on her nightstand until the day she died.

better? I want you to keep me informed about your condition if you don't mind. Remember Dad has done much general medicine including obstetrics & you know how deeply & affectionately interested I am ... ¶ ... Akin working in my office for a month this summer. He gave every evidence of having a high order of intelligence, dependability & resourcefulness. All very pleasing to us all. Bill was elected student advisor.. upper third of class. ¶ What do you think of the freight trains of the air Rog? I know much of the inside of the matter as I am examining the eyes of our officers. They expect so they say, to have a plane out for London every 15 minutes & one in from there every 15 min.!! Megalomania I believe is the appellation! Keep it to yourself.

AUGUST 1942. GRANDMA TO ROGER.

Dearest Roger and Gerry, Have been here (at Vonhurst) just a week — the same old place — very peaceful — cool — really quite cold several days. Have had a fire going almost every day but today is warm, 78 degrees to be exact and most comfortable. We do wish that you both could have been with us — Shenna *(Sheldon)* too — I think North Carolina has been hotter than he expected *(Sheldon doing summer study at UNC)*. ... Our days here are so simple — Dad of course is studying and writing a paper to be read this October. We get up at 7:30, Dad a half hour earlier in order to get the underbrush off his ? . After breakfast Akin and I go for a row. He rows one way and I row on the return trip. I don't think there is a rock along the shore that we have not investigated. Are usually gone 2 hours — then I go for a swim. Akin and Dad sit on the beach — they say it is <u>too</u> cold. It is a little chilly at first but really wonderful. Then ? — read a bit — the paper comes in at 11:30 and then to lunch — which I shouldn't eat but do. Dad then takes a nap until three. He is sawing wood, but will arise about three-thirty, walk to Center harbor for the exercise. I only go as far as the Von's place but Adie *(Akin)* is a good fellow and goes with Dad. I think Dad is almost rested — in another week he will be anxious to return to the office. Helen and Bill arrive tomorrow ... Vivian writes that Washington has had a terrific rain storm which cooled the air but almost flooded the place. ... Dear Gerry, we hope the terrific heat has let up and that you are quite comfortable. I have been so sorry that you have been miserable, We all send our love.

Affectionately, Mother

AUGUST 29, 1942. GRANDPA TO ROGER (5 LONG PAGES). EXCERPTS:

(Missed you in New Hampshire.) Mr. Von would have taken you to a private estate where he has the privilege of some excellent trout fishing ... Know Gerry that our Rog is quite an expert trout fisherman. Like everything else he does he does it well. ¶ *(Bill has another 2 years in medical training ... Sheldon enlisting into service when he returns from UNC)* ¶ We are very proud of you son on your marks in the course. It makes us happy to see you progressing & making the same good name for yourself that will follow you all through life ... It will mean a lot on his record & that is a good thing. I feel sure he will distinguish himself in the Army & be outstanding as he has been since he was in the first grade." ¶ *(Akin going into his senior year in high school and is interested in going to Princeton — Grandpa would like for him to talk to Roger, a Princeton grad, and would send him by Pullman train to California in early September before school starts) ... (talk with him)* spur his ambitions. He will enter ROTC & also the premedical course & that will I think hold him in the university & allow him to get his education. These boys without an education after the war will have very stiff going. Akin is too fine a lad to have such a handicap. He has an excellent mind son. Not a smart alec which pleases me as you know. His mind is logical & meticulous & hence not <u>fast</u> & superficial. He is the quietest youngster I have ever known but he never misses a trick. The very happy faculty of having his eyes & ears open and his mouth shut. 'Shut your mouth & save your life.' Be sure & say if it is not convenient for Akin to come now.

SEPTEMBER 6, 1942. GRANDPA TO ROGER (12 PAGES). EXCERPTS:

(Akin) admires you Rog & loves & admires you both Gerry. What you have to say will influence him a great deal ... He is an unusual lad; so very quiet & of such few words that he isn't easy to know. Beneath this outer calm there is a fine & strong character. I will appreciate your hospitality & advice to him very deeply for it will in this crucial time of his life, have a great deal of influence ... ¶ Gerry darling your last letter is a jewel of great price. We cannot tell you how much we enjoyed it and how deeply we appreciate it ... *(Rog)*, she is a comfort & joy. Let me say here and now that during the vicissitudes of these times of stress that Mother & my chief desire is to have a home for our daughters, their children & our sons. Here is room, love, & home for them & their children. A yard fenced in, a big

house & bigger hearts to welcome them. Gerry you will know this is genuine & from the heart if & when you wish to come to us; for little time, for long time, for as long as you wish & desire. Rog beloved son of my heart, of our hearts, have no fear but that as long as darling Mother and I have life our home is yours & your family too. To love & to cherish so long as we may live. I am too old to longer serve in war. To love, serve & support those who are in it is about all we can do. To do this for our boys & their families is a loving & sacred duty and one that can only give us the deepest joy & satisfaction. Son & daughter when I came to spell vicissitude I had to call to <u>Akin</u> to bring out Webster!! Not so hot as I might be on spelling!! ...

SEPTEMBER 20, 1942. GRANDPA TO ROGER (11 LONG PAGES). EXCERPTS:
.. I have had to abandon my trip to Dayton en route to Chicago. I am asked to sit with the American Board of Ophthalmology on September 8.9 & 10. I am on the program on September 11,12,13,& 14. On one of those days I have to broadcast over the National hook up ... will come in a few weeks.. ¶ ... I cannot imagine myself a grandad but I shall be like the rest of them — daffy, quite! ¶ Rog, John Pratt was in the office yesterday, he goes into the Marines shortly. Richard is Gunnery Officer on the Destroyer Lansdowne: a brand new ship. John said 'he got two of Hitler's subs. Has been commended for the one & will shortly be commended for the other!' Some boy Dick. ¶ We thank you for being so nice to Akin. The trip & visit with you meant a great deal to him. He is devoted to you both ... ¶ *(Concerning Col. Hopkins:)* I think it just as well perhaps if you did not see him. I think he like all bureau chiefs a pirate. Naturally he wants the good ones. I would too & so I would want you ... ¶ ..Saturday next he (Sheldon) enlists. Rog my son my old heart is sad that he didn't take advantage of his opportunities. May our dear Lord grant to Mother & me & to you his brothers that his ambition will awaken. Beneath he is a fine man. Courage, will, intelligence and <u>character</u>. It will show forth in time but <u>now</u> is the time to get an education without which he will be in dire straits after this period is over. ¶ *(Grandpa has told Roger to send him the bill for the photographs many times and he grows restless)* Rog: General Orders no 11 HdQrs. dated Sept 20, 1942. 1st Lt. Roger HB. Davis will forward without delay the bill for the photographs of his wife & himself to his Commanding Officer. By command of Renée T. Davis Commanding General. William T. Davis, adjt. For failure to comply with an order see Article of war 37!!! It will be invoked!!!

❡ Gerry ... you <u>do</u> write such wonderful letters daughter. Our Rog is doing the usual, making friends everywhere ... he has that capacity as you have. .You complement each other perfectly ... may joy be yours & your childrens & may Mother and I live long to enjoy it with you. I hope Gerry dear that I shall be fortunate enough to meet & know your father & to know better your lovely mother. Mother and I love her even after the very short acquaintance we had. ❡ ... *(Roger)* has been a comfort & joy to us since he first saw the light of day. May I tell you what the Headmaster of Friends School said when he graduated & went to Princeton. 'Doctor he will be a great comfort to you.' ... his prophecy came true & was true before that time.

OCTOBER 6, 1942. GRANDPA TO ROGER (7 LONG PAGES). EXCERPTS:
Includes Dart crash report and discusses the incident.

... Carefully keep this report; it will guard you from a suit since this is federal evidence in an official report. Very interesting. ❡ .. Just as I was sitting down to write you our Kentucky cousins many times removed came in; hence the pyramids! They are great great grandchildren of Dr. Graham. Figure out the relationship if you can. Name is Don. He is Princeton '42; you were there together. His sister goes to the Porter School near Farmington Conn. ..The lad is a Captain in Intelligence. Very fine pair of youngsters. He is married — N. J. girl, live wire; they have a healthy 5 mo. old. Their father died. Mother remarried. Taylor ? live in Montrose (we belong to the Clan Montrose) near Louisville KY — so much for family history — you may meet him in the service. 'Blood is thicker than water' ... ❡
The profound last paragraph of this letter:

... Cheerio my darlings; my dearly beloved daughter & son. God grant we may soon be together again. I remember Gerry my dear old Grandmother used to say as the end drew nigh, 'Soon I shall go where there are no more partings'; as the circle nears completion my thoughts revert to her counsel (my mother died when I was very young) and her counsel was so good, so wise and so lasting. 'We shall all meet on that nether shore where partings are no more' she used to say. ... Good night dear 'children'

Devotedly always, Dad

OCTOBER 20, 1942. LAST LETTER FROM ROGER THAT WE COULD FIND. IN ITS ENTIRETY,

Dear Mom & Dad, I have been meaning to send the enclosed chart ever since it was published but kept forgetting to bring a copy of it home. From looking at it and also the ink chart I made I believe you can see where my little 'cog' fits into the picture. ¶ Dad, I just read your letter concerning the dinner party we could give for Gen Vanaman, Col. Hargreaves, etc. I wonder if it would be the best thing to do? Gen V. is away from his home so much; business trips, dinners, parties, speeches, etc. Perhaps when he gets a chance to be at home he really enjoys it. As for the rest of the folks I think it would be very nice. Sunday evening at the Van Cleve Hotel is always quite nice. You remember we ate there with Ralph Fehr when you were here before. ¶ Gerry and I want to thank you so much for making us a present of our own pictures. We really wanted some very badly and are very pleased with them. ¶ Everything is going fine here. Work is hard and sometimes long but I enjoy it. ¶ Gerry is feeling very well but tires easily. However, a few hours rest and she is full of energy again. Once in a while she has an uncomfortable day but not very often. ¶ Our new apartment had its roof completed today so we actually believe there is some hope of moving in before Christmas. ¶ I imagine Sheldon is on his way by now. Best of luck to him. I know the Army will do him a lot of good and I have no doubt but that he will do the Army some good. I have faith in him as we all do. Gerry and I will be so interested to hear what he does and how he progresses. ¶ We surely are looking forward to your visit, Dad. I don't go to work until 8:00 a.m. or after now so it might be a good idea for me to meet you at the station. We could have breakfast and go on out to the Field. Or would you rather rest a bit first. Whatever you prefer?

Love to all, Rog

OCTOBER 21, 1942. GRANDMA TO ROGER. EXCERPTS:

It has been such a long time since I have written but Dad has been good at writing his marvelous epistles. ¶ First of all I meant to tell you how delighted I am to hear about the new bedroom set. I wanted to tell you to get a new one but I was afraid you might think I was butting in. The dishes too must be a great addition to the cupboard. Now what have you in the way of silverware? Good silver plate is very scarce but perhaps we can find some. ¶ Bill is still pegging away. His last day of obstetrical duty is over. I believe he helped ten or more babies into the world — all colored as he is was in a colored clinic ... I have been so engrossed in my thoughts of Sheldon these past weeks I haven't been able to concentrate on anything; so excuse scrawl and spelling ... He was sworn in today as a private — passed his physical yesterday. He is at Fort McClellan, Anniston, AL ... The tetanus serum the doctors give the soldiers as they enter the service has most of the horse element taken out ... God bless the boy for his courage, guts and will to do ... ¶ ... We are parting with one of our spare tires. The Packard has two you know and we are allowed only one spare ... ¶ ..We had a dinner party last Saturday night ... This Saturday afternoon Dad is having a few officers in for mint juleps — General Arnold, General Ulio. Col. Lull, Medical Corps, etc. ... ¶ .. The furnace is now a coal burner and I can tell you we miss the oil ... If we don't put in coal the blame thing goes out and if we do put in coal we nearly burn up. You know Dad and his saying he must have air. About two o'clock this morning the furnace burned up and we were lying about with only a sheet on. Dad rushes to the basement — opens and shuts and pulls everything except the fire alarm — <u>nothing</u> did any good. The office still has oil although a notice came today that we would have 75% of what was used last year ... ¶ We have almost given up sending wedding presents. I just can't send to everyone. Literally we have received dozens of wedding invitations ... ¶ What a long, long wait isn't it Gerry? It is the longest nine months in ones life. Cheer up, it takes an elephant eleven years! ... ¶ Want Adie Boy to mail this before he goes to bed so must close.

My fondest love to my dear children, Affectionately, Mother

NOVEMBER 15, 1942. GRANDPA TO ROGER (11 PAGES). EXCERPTS:

We had such a nice visit from Bill & Helen & such a nice visit over the telephone with you fellows. Wasn't that grand. We have just returned from the station (7 pm) seeing them off to Baltimore ... Bill has been working very hard ... both look well; Helen provides good food & lots of it which has seen Bill through the hard places. She is a wonderful wife Gerry just as you are & we love you two daughters dearly for yourselves and for the devotion to duty & to your husbands ... ¶ I was in Richmond VA on Wednesday & Thursday having a paper to read to the eye section. Went out to see 'Uncle Jamie' General Jammisson ... He is I fear upon his death bed & it wrung my heart. He sends his fondest love to you and Gerry & his congratulations upon the future arrival. I saw so many of my friends of the South & my paper was exceedingly well received & discussed with all the seriousness & courtesy so characteristic of the men of that section. I have two more papers to deliver, one in December in New York City in conjunction with the

American Board of Ophthalmology; also in New York City before the NY Academy of Ophthalmology on war injuries to the eyes, their prevention & treatment. Then I am through — for the moment ...

NOVEMBER 22, 1942. GRANDPA TO ROGER (5 PAGES). EXCERPTS:
..This Thanksgiving will be the smallest family gathering we have ever had. Only darling Mother, Akin and myself ... ¶ Rog you are a busy man but I am going to ask just a little of your time to write once a week to Sheldon. ..He is a grain of sand on the seashore — one of 7.5 millions ... The boy worked out his place there all by himself. I had nothing to do with it whatsoever. ..connected with the Riverside Academy & know him. He has every advantage in being selected for the officers training school & I think will make good. The Divine Spark has been ignited. He will go onward & upward & barring accidents I think we shall hear of him. No happiness can be so deep to our darling Mother and to me as the happiness and success of our sons. Bill & you have made good & will so continue. Sheldon will so do the same. Akin is the same steady & conscientious student. Honest, fearless, capable. All our sons are Men. We have given much to our Country in you four. You will leave your mark upon it. ¶ Gerry darling I know you impatiently wait The Day! A bit of a hard grind isn't it daughter but the happiness that awaits you (and us) will recompense you for it all & in a few days it will be forgotten in the joy of little clasping hands and loving eyes. 'Tis God's greatest gift to the world — 'suffer little children, to come unto me, and forbid them not for of such is the Kingdom of Heaven' and well might it be. Our thoughts are with you constantly ... ¶ It cheers me son to hear you are looking after your physical self. It pays great dividends. Then, too you must set the example to your kiddy..

DECEMBER 16, 1942. GRANDPA TO ROGER (6 PAGES). EXCERPTS:
Just back from NY. Hard work and a few pleasant incidents ... I sat with the American Board of Ophthalmology examining candidates for efficiency.. The travel from N.Y., Philadelphia & points south from there is exceedingly heavy. Great swarms of people. Long long trains hours late. Stations jammed full of people. Soldiers, sailors, marines and civilians. White, yellow and brown. Bags, parents, babies, kiddies, old folks but all in a good humor. Americans are wonderful that way. Almost every one trying to help others less strong & less fortunate. When Mother got off the train in Dayton

a young officer carried her suitcase for her. She probably told you. I examined men (doctors) from Vermont to the Panama Canal, California & China! Most interesting. One man flew from China to take the exam … I was so interested to hear all about you two from Mother. Almost like a visit with you. I wish I could have been there too but my life like yours Rog requires constant attention to the job. Perhaps I may see you in the early spring and greet little Rog or Rogina. ¶ *(speaking to Gerry about his sons)* … Gerry they are a great solace and comfort to us as your & Roger's children will be to you. 'Tis the greatest source of happiness we have in the world. 'He (or she) who has children never dies.' This is a proverb of the Arabs of the desert of Arabia I picked up long ago in that bitter though fascinating edge of the world. I think of you constantly Gerry dear. I know you have uncomfortable days. But what a recompense. Be cheerful!.. you are young & strong and the time of travail will be short and easy. Have no fear darling daughter, all will be well. It is the natural order of things that God in his wisdom hath ordained. His blessing will be upon yours and ours also. you are the blessed of earth — you young mothers. The most beautiful sight that man has beheld is the young mother with her babe in her arms — you are all madonnas and are the blessing & joy of all men. May our Dear Lord bless & keep you and yours — as he will.

Devotedly Dad

Akin wrote a note at the end of the letter, … Just got back from school where I took my last term exam. I don't have to go back until January 5th … The draft is right in our backyard now. Several boys at school have had their preliminary physical examinations and have been classified as 1-A. Quite a few have registered and I don't know how long it will be before some are actually inducted.

Love, Akin

December 20, 1942. Grandpa to Roger (3 pages). Excerpts:

(Christmas apart) … we shall be with you in spirit. May it be a happy day for you on your first Christmas together and may there be many of them with a happy family circle about you such as we have had these many years. The memory of them will be about your dear mother and me like an incense for all time … We shall call you on the telephone next Sunday (27th) so as not to use the wires on Christmas day that our soldier boys may have the right of way. We hope Sheldon may be able to talk with us that day. Will you return Sheldon's letter at once so we can have it for Bill & Helen

to read. It was such a fine letter & Bill like yourself is so deeply interested in the boy. He makes our hearts swell with joy & pride at his manliness & courage. Not a word of complaint and he is having it <u>tough & hard</u>. It will do him no harm but will strengthen & mold his fiber. Something he needs really. As you know Rog he has a <u>very strong</u> character and a powerful will.

DECEMBER 25, 1942. GRANDPA TO ROGER (3 PAGES). EXCERPTS:
... we had a telephone call *(on Christmas day)* from Sheldon in Atlanta. He was at Col. Bragdon's home. Dorothy ('Duty') Col. B's daughter is Sheldon's dearly beloved. They are really very fond of each other. She is a girl of fine character; a dandy girl whom we love dearly. Col. B..stationed in Atlanta ... have taken Sheldon to their hearts and to their home ... drop him a note quite often. He holds you in high regard & esteem & a word from you will mean much to him. Do this for the love we bear you ... having your letter & Sheldon's telephone conversation made the day so satisfactory, so replete with happiness knowing all our loved ones were happy. Gerry darling daughter, your letters are so lovely and so sweet. You endear yourself to us more & more ... We honor and esteem your father and mother in rearing such a fine girl of such character. And so we thank our dear Lord and Jesus of Nazareth for the happiness He has visited upon us dear daughter in you. Greatly blessed are we this Christmas day, so greatly blessed ...
Notes/letters from Bill, Helen, Akin and Grandma enclosed.

DECEMBER 26, 1942. GRANDPA TO ROGER (3 PAGES). EXCERPTS:
We did appreciate your Christmas gifts so much. My weakness for hankies is so well known to you. ¶ There was a great to-do on the River today; a very low ceiling something around 400 feet but good visibility. The big bombers were roaring from before daylight until dark tonight & heavy explosions far down the River from time to time. Just what it was all about I do not know. We saw one that came below the ceiling high tailing it for the landing field ...

DECEMBER 30, 1942. GRANDMA TO ROGER & GERRY. EXCERPTS:
Just two weeks and a day since I left you. So much has been doing and so many things have happened that it seems much longer. I did have such a nice visit with you both and so enjoyed being with you — It was a joy to me to see you both so happy and so nicely settled. You have made a real

start in life and a good one. It made me happy to be made so comfortably at home ... ¶ Rog I was disappointed that your real present didn't arrive — Dad gave you a fine gabardine trench coat. *(See photo on page 172.)* Dondero didn't have your size so ordered one. It has not come but is expected. I was afraid if we sent the check you would spend the money for other things. <u>When</u> it arrives if it isn't right send it back. Or better still if you promise to get the good coat there I will send the check. Don't get those at $40.00 they are not all wool — these others are $65.00 are beautiful. ¶ Sheldon's phone call on Christmas just made the day for me. I missed the lad so and my heart was heavy — all the week before I had worried about him — had him in my mind and heart. His letter arrived on Christmas also, and it told of having been ill for a week. Finally reported as he couldn't crawl an-

Roger in Roger and Gerry's apartment during or soon after Renée's stay in December 1942.

other step. He got twenty four hours off, not in the infirmary but back in his barracks. Via the grape-vine through General Lynch..Sheldon was doing well, stood well with his officers etc. Before going to Preparatory Camp for the O.C.S. he is to be put in charge of a company as a enlisted instructor — This is what is known as a cadre. The duty is eight weeks. This will not please Sheldon as he is most anxious to get to O.C.S ..also he is to take a radio course ...

JANUARY 3, 1943. GRANDPA TO ROGER (6 PAGES). EXCERPTS:
.. Bill & Helen & Henry Clark & his wife went to the Chevy Chase Club New years Eve & rolled in at 6 am. Akin went to a private party & arrived home at 6:30 am. I was up as per usual at 4:30 a.m. but I noted they 'snuck' into their rooms without saying good morning. They thought I was fixing the furnace!! We have switched from oil to coal. ¶ Akin has gotten to be something of a roue'!!! Last night he was invited to a party for dinner and afterwards a dance at the Sulgrave Club, arriving home this a.m. at 3. We are happy to have him get about — you will understand this Rog. He is a good boy but he needs just this sort of thing. Isn't it fine that our boy Sheldon has found himself. He has very fine and very strong characteristics, a will of iron, a charming personality and a determination so strong and no sense of fear. Barring bad breaks he may make an outstanding career in the Army. Unless I am biased, having such great love for my sons and their mother, I really believe he has the attributes of a great soldier. A throwback to our Highland ancestors ... ¶ .. Bill graduates in medicine March 25.. he has an internship at Johns Hopkins. After that the army. He was a Cooch Artillery Reserve Officer, after entering medicine was made a 2nd Lieutenant MAC *(Medical Administrative Corps)* and will be made a 1st Lt. Med Corps upon completing his hospital training.. He has worked so hard these 4 years and Helen has backed him like a good fellow. We are so fortunate oh so fortunate, in our dearly beloved daughters-in-law. We always think of them as our daughters, <u>not</u> the in-laws since they are just as dear to us as our own daughters. Sheldon's girl Dorothy Bragdon, is a fine splendid girl too. I do hope they will be married when he has his commission. She is a real girl: no smoking & drinking and plenty of character just as Gerry & Helen. May our dear Lord bless them and may we have plenty of grandchildren to give to our country more men and women of true worth and character. ¶ Doesn't Shenna write interesting letters. You will note how graphic

they are and how they depict before your imagination what he is doing. It is a gift — he has it in marked degree. Rog, you will be deeply pleased at Bill's development. He has gifted talents too and barring accidents will go to the top. All of our sons have the ability to hitch their wagons to a star. Our Rog has it in large degree hasn't he Gerry? I'll say he has and doesn't it make us happy. Good night my dears & God be with you.

Ever devotedly, Dad

JANUARY 23, 1943.
Roger promoted to Captain, Army Air Forces (they were still referring to him in his official papers as Captain, Air Corps).

JANUARY 31, 1943. GRANDPA TO ROGER (8 PAGES). EXCERPTS:
.. Rog dear son see that Gerry has ? ; a <u>good</u> room — the best is not too good. Everything that safety & comfort requires and send us the bills or pay them promptly & send us the receipted bills so we may send you a check. When the Dr. sends his bill <u>you</u> pay it and advise us what it is & we will send you check to cover. Genl Orders No. 11 dated Army HdQrs. January 31, 1943. Obey it or be shot (or half shot at dawn!). Seriously Rog beloved son this is your mother's & my pleasure & happiness to do this. Please permit us this happiness. You will won't you? The old folks at home will be made much happier if we have your assurance that you will do this. We want dear Gerry to have all assurances of safety & comfort in her time of travail — a happy, normal travail to bring into the world a child so greatly beloved & cherished our first grandchild & we are prepared to love him or her with all the love that we have for Gerry & for you ... Four times have our dear mother had this delight and there is nothing in this life that gives the joy and heartfelt satisfaction. Rog,..be not afraid. Your beloved will come through with no hurt. Some pain yes, this the will of God, but woman is prepared for this by nature.. your dear sweet young wife is physically & mentally strong. She is but carrying out her mission in life. To give the world, to our nation a child who will live to be a comfort & joy to you both & to us and an honor to his country ... Rog, would that I could be with you in these hours that I have suffered four times & when our four sons were being born. Have faith my son; have courage. Gerry will have no trouble. Call me on the telephone during those hours — from the hospital. Just as often as you wish — it cannot be too often. Let me be with you. If you wish me to be there tell me so & I will

come & be with you ... ❡ Gerry my darling daughter be not afraid. Thy fate is the common fate of all of the devoted wives & mothers who made this nation great. Your confinement will be normal and safe and easy. The pains of motherhood are not too severe. I have been in attendance on so many. It is not hard, not too difficult. You are young; you are strong, you are happy in the thought of having a child which all of us share with you. In a few hours all will be well & so many of us will be happy with you. Every hour I shall be thinking of you — of our dear Rog. Should I be needed I shall catch the first plane & be with you & our dear Rog in a few hours. But that will not occur my darling. You will need no assistance from anyone. And so be of stout hearts, brave & assured. Your motherhood soon to be will be so happy and so joyous that the few pains of a normal labor will be nothing. They are not bad to a strong & healthy girl like yourself. You have what it takes — be not afraid. It is a normal procedure, nothing more. ❡ To both of you — my beloved daughter & son, do not be apprehensive or have any fear; all will be well & we shall toast our first grandchild on the 25th of March here in the old home, to a long and happy life in which we shall all share with a heart full of love. ❡ Good night beloved children of mine; I know God in His Heaven watches over two and three of His children & showers His love & Benediction upon you.

Again good night & with all of my love believe me ever & always your devoted Dad

FEBRUARY 7, 1943. GRANDPA TO ROGER (3 PAGES). EXCERPTS:

... Gerry dear the long wait is about over.. ❡ ... Akin is fine & such a good student. Poor lad, his educational days will be sadly interfered with. We cannot decide as yet where he had best go to college. It is quite a problem. The new regulations are out concerning the 18 year old draftees. He will be 18 next October.

FEBRUARY 14, 1943. GRANDPA TO ROGER (3 PAGES). EXCERPTS:

We think of you tonight and are with you in spirit: tense hours these.. Fear not my beloved ones all will be well & we shall all be so happy. You Gerry darling, will be the happiest of all when you cuddle your baby to your heart; Rog will be next. The most beautiful picture since the beginning of man is the lovely young mother with her babe pressed close to her heart, I can see as if yesterday our beloved mother holding you boys so; 'tis of the es-

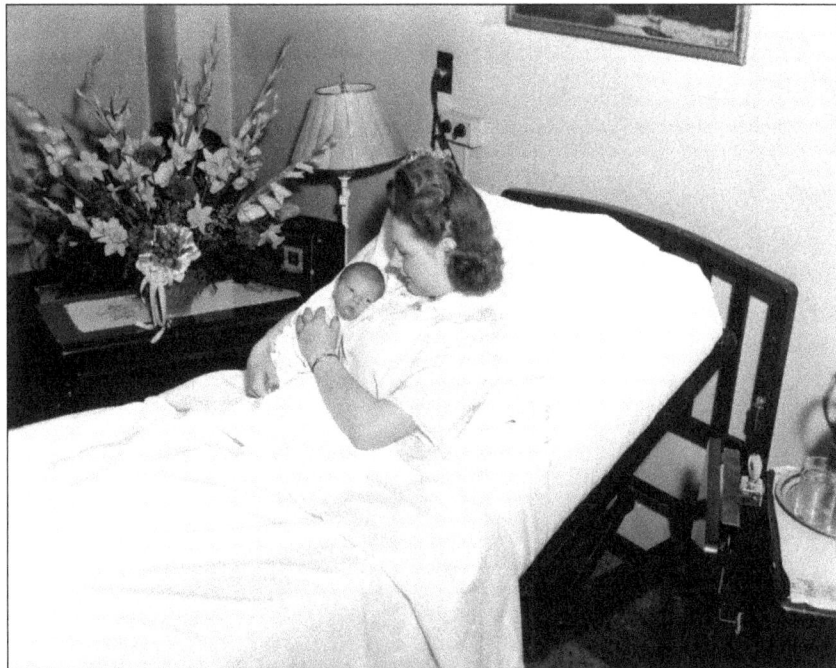

February 21, 1943: Gerry with Rogie, five days old, Good Samaritan Hospital, Dayton, Ohio.

sence of God. 'Bring little children unto me & forbid them not, for of such is the Kingdom of Heaven.' This to me is the most beautiful thing ever uttered by the tongue of man. ¶ ... Sheldon's letters come regularly.. giving him tough training ... Bill is grinding hard. Akin studies into the late hours.. Mother darling is fine and I am the same old tough Dad who loves you with all my heart. I am now passed my 66th year. Engaging life working harder than I ever did & keenly alive to the well being & success of my sons & daughters.

FEBRUARY 16, 1943.
Roger's first son born. Roger HB. Davis, Jr. born in a private hospital in Dayton (Wright Field did not have a hospital). Grandma Huber goes to help them during this period (stays 1 or 2 months).

MARCH 15, 1943. GRANDPA TO BABY "ROGY" (3 PAGES). EXCERPT:
Dearest Rogy, And so you will be 4 weeks old tomorrow and weigh 9

lbs.+. <u>Some boy</u>. I know you are a happy family now and we wish we could peek in and see you some evening before you are tucked in for the night. ¶ Sheldon is ordered to the officers training school at Fort Benning Ga leaving Fort McClellan ...

MARCH 21, 1943. GRANDPA TO ROGER (5 PAGES). EXCERPTS:

... Col. Bissel is leaving shortly for Fort Sill Oklahoma — the artillery school. An enormous post now. He was in the office yesterday and asked to be remembered to you. He looks very badly; long hard hours at a desk; no exercise; no recreation. Please take note — NO exercise!! He is going to duty with troops & is very happy about it, as I am for him for life at a desk for a Regular is poison — cold poison ...

MARCH 25, 1943.

Bill (William Joseph Graham Davis) graduates from University of Maryland Medical school.

MARCH 28, 1943. GRANDPA TO ROGER (5 PAGES). EXCERPT:

... Gerry, Rog, if that boy (Rogy) is red headed he is mine. I longed for a red head like his grandmother had when each of my four sons arrived. No luck ...

APRIL 18, 1943. GRANDPA TO ROGER (4 LONG PAGES). EXCERPTS:

.. We can see in our imagination your happy home, filled with love and serene happiness. This happiness my small son is the greatest gift God has given us and it radiates across the miles as does light, instantaneously ... Our Gerry is a busy & happy little person bless her darling little heart. I can see her singing in her heart about her duties as mother, wife and devoted friend & teacher. Son you will have appreciated by now how much of life these loving wives teach us. As Robert Louis Stevenson said of his wife: lover, friend and teacher. A man without such a wife knows only a modicum of what life can hold.. Rog, son aren't we fortunate? To have such companions, such pals, such loyal & devoted friends, such a part of our hearts and our souls, your dear wife and mine. Thank Almighty God for them. Nor gold, nor weather, nor social position weigh in the balance with them. They are the essence of our Lord.. Helen ..such a grand girl..they too are a source of happiness to us all.. 'The Squire' *(Sheldon)* is making good.. Dorothy..too is a real girl, fine and womanly.. As the slanting rays of the setting sun of life cast shadows upon the screen of the nether world we are very happy in our daughters and sons & their children. We thank our Dear Lord that life has been so full of happiness for us. For our happiness rests in you dear children. 'He that hath children (like you) never dies' says the Turkish Proverb. We live on in you ... Gerry daughter I am so proud & happy that you can nurse your son. Rog the most beautiful thing in all this world — the most spiritual: the Madonna & her child. You have it in Gerry as I did in your mother. To see her with boys at her breast was the most wonderful sight that human eyes may behold; the most sacred ...

APRIL 25, 1943. GRANDPA TO ROGER (7 PAGES). EXCERPTS:

Gerry, darling daughter, how wonderful your letter.. We have read and re-read today your dear letter. May I compliment you as an old soldier of many campaigns on your discipline. The military defini-

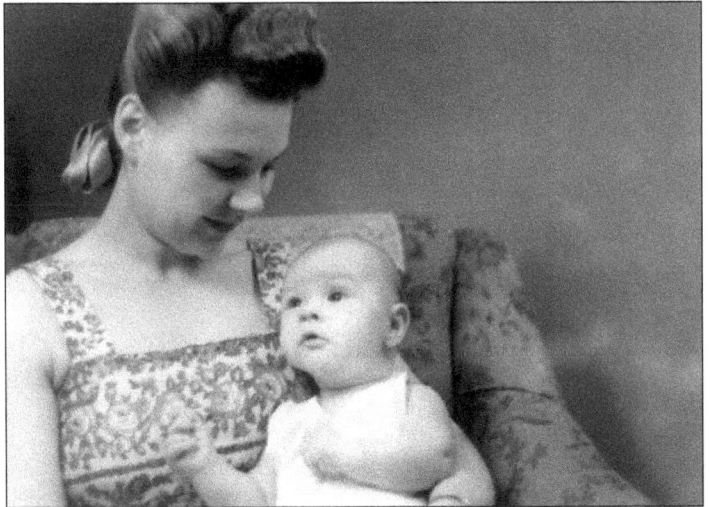

Gerry (TOP) and Gerry and Rogie when he was 15 weeks old.

tion of discipline being 'doing the same thing at the same time each day.' Thus your son will be the happy recipient of discipline & you are giving him

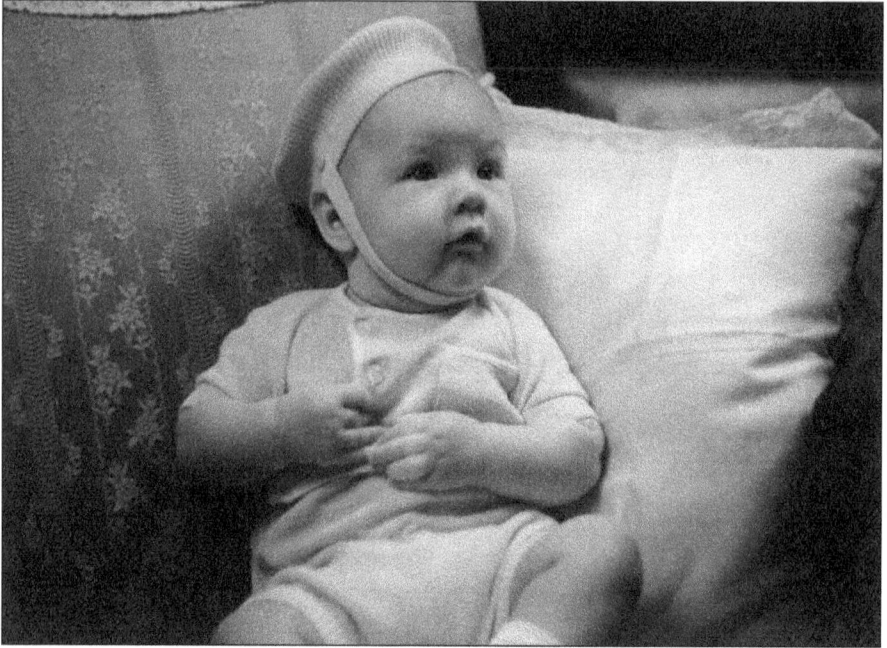

Rogie at 15 weeks.

in his first weeks of life an advantage that is not measured in words. ¶ Gerry daughter can't you send out the laundry? At least part of it.. Mother tells me there is no more ? work. Please daughter do this; mother and I will be so very happy to see to the financial side of it. It is not well to leave a small baby alone It is not well for a nursing mother to spend much time in a basement (this from a doctor of 42 years experience), It is not well darling for you to work <u>too</u> hard while nursing a splendid vigorous boy. You give him much; oh so much ... *Roger, Gerry and Rogie coming to Washington 1st of May for visit.*

APRIL 30, 1943. GRANDPA TO ROGER (2 PAGES). EXCERPT:
What joy to think we are to have you under our roof again in two weeks. I am taking that week off for vacation to enjoy with you.. We will be at the station to meet you. Let us know the car you are in and we will be at the train to help with all the things & with the 'King,' our Rog ...

SUNDAY, MAY 9, 1943. GRANDPA TO ROGER (4 PAGES). EXCERPTS:
Dearest beloved children, We had such a happy visit with Bill. He and

I talked hours on ophthalmology and other hours on the joy of seeing you three. We spent the day at the Glen.. Bill (and I) sat under the trees and talked shop for hours in the perfect quiet of the deep countryside but 30 minutes drive from our house here. Bill left at 5 o'clock.. Darling mother found this lovely place. We gardened: planting potatoes, corn, beans, etc etc. in ground which had been ploughed, harrowed & rolled. Beautiful soil is rich & loamy. I found I had much reserve strength & feel so fine tonight for the exercise. This children three is a 'Haven for Refuge' from the 'other people' in the edge of the city but deep in the country. Darling mother and I planned to have it so for our children and for us ...

MAY 30, 1943. GRANDPA TO ROGER (5 PAGES). EXCERPTS:
... Rogie's rosy mouth, big intelligent eyes, big strong body and warming ways! He captures our hearts completely. How nice to visit with you Gerry & Rog. To take you in our hearts again. To hold our grandson close to our hearts & see him smile up at us. To see the daily development like the opening of a rose bud in the sun. 'Suffer little children to come unto me, & forbid them not for of such is the Kingdom of Heaven.' To my mind the most beautiful words that have been spoken on this earth.. ¶ .. Akin's commencement.. Akin rolled in at 4 a.m. this morning. Getting it all out of his system as have his 3 brothers before him. Just as well to let them blow it off young son & daughter. With a good home training & absorbing the true values of life therefrom & being welcomed home no matter what the hour one need have no fear.. ¶ Gerry daughter if our Rog should be suddenly ordered away hop the train for Washington with our boy Rogie. Make your plans from here. Stay with us as long as you wish & go to your home in Montana when you desire ... rent your home furnished..by the month..

JUNE 12, 1943. GRANDPA TO ROGER (4 PAGES). EXCERPTS:
.. Remember the family motto — all for one & one for all. There were really 4 of the musketeers you know. ¶ I am to read a paper in Mexico City in August but doubt if I can get there. Only if I can fly will I go. This is doubtful. Also I am invited to read several papers in Rio de Janeiro in Nov '43 but I am sure I cannot get there. It would take 2.5 weeks to go by surface transportation & cost a thousand dollars to go by air. Not me. The papers will be sent to be read however. I have worked all day today since six o'clock this a.m. on the Mexico paper — it is now 10 p.m. & so good night

my beloved children. Hold my little Rogie close & kiss him for me. Would I could look into his eyes tonight. What is the color now? ..

MONDAY, JULY 5, 1943. GRANDPA TO ROGER (4 PAGES). EXCERPT
Sheldon graduating from the infantry O.C.S. at Fort Benning and taking the train to Washington for a week's leave.
... How wonderful it is that Rog will come (for the weekend) & see his brother. The 4 of them will be here & it will no doubt be a long time before that happens again ...

WEEKEND OF JULY 10, 1943 —
All four boys home.

JULY 18, 1943 — GRANDPA TO ROGER (7 PAGES). EXCERPTS:
.. has been pretty bad here; street temperatures of 105 degrees & that is <u>hot</u>. Mother dear is planning to go to Vonhurst July 29 for which I am glad. She really suffers with the heat and I think it really bad for her. She will remain through August and a while into September I hope. Children <u>do you need</u> the air conditioner? We don't really need it and if you do please let us send it to you. Rog boy I asked Mother to send you a check for your trip. I appreciate your generosity dear son in not wishing to take it but it has long been agreed that when children come home it gives us such great joy & pleasure & satisfaction that we consider it a privilege to bear the expense.. ¶ We talked to Sheldon this morning. He reported for duty Friday July 16. Goes on a hundred mile hike starting tomorrow a.m. with negro troops. I should say this is a good set up since they are usually amenable to discipline when officered by whites & particular southerners. Sheldon said as soon as he spoke with his southern accent they immediately assigned him to this duty. This will be his first experience as an officer commanding troops and it will be novel & exciting for him.. He gained 5 lbs. when he was at home. He was as thin as a rail when arrived.. The only sad note was not having you and Rogie. We missed you so much. Mother and I are quite gaga about Rogie. We declared that we wouldn't be a bore about him to our friends but we are. I tease mother by saying she carries his photograph about with her & stops the postman on the streets & shows it to him!! But really daughter I think we are fairly sane considering how proud we are of him and his beauty & strength. He is a wonderful child & such wonderful eyes and strong body &

high I.Q. He has it all and why shouldn't he. Look at his mother & his Dad and his 4 grandparents! Boy we hate ourselves don't we? ¶ The war looks good doesn't it. I was greatly pleased at what Churchill & Roosevelt told Italy. They will take heed if they can get out of the yoke which Mussolini & Hitler have them in ... ¶ This moment (4 p.m.) a telegram from Sheldon; is ordered to Camp Gruber (named after one of my buddies) Okla. to report for duty with the Rainbow (42nd Division), a <u>choice</u> assignment. Selah!! If you want some thrills read the military history of this Division.*

AUGUST 7, 1943 — GRANDPA TO ROGER (4 PAGES). EXCERPTS:
   Have thought of you a lot this week & hoped the weather has not been too hot. It has been fiercely hot here. The whole day & night hot, ? and incandescent — **for 38 days**. Crops all burning up, wells drying up, cattle suffering. It is **very bad** ... ¶ Yesterday Yoley Maddux was in the office and asked all about you all.. she said that Cabell was in Command of a Landing Ship Tank: a 350 foot vessel. He was part of the invasion force of Italy. His ship had knocked several planes of the enemy out of the air..

AUGUST 15, 1943. GRANDPA TO ROGER (2 LONG PAGES). EXCERPTS:
   .. This summer for the first time there have been nights when it did not cool off outside!! I have seen it at Aden (Arabia — entrance to the Red Sea) where the temperatures stayed around 110 degrees all night with not a breath stirring & it had not rained in 20 years!! ... I have written Ralph Fehr about a cooler; he may know of one that can be had. This will be our present to Rogie but you two can share it with him — Joke. Hope I can find one. I am too slow. Should have thought about it <u>before</u> the summer not when it is about over.

AUGUST 29, 1943. GRANDPA TO ROGER (4 LONG PAGES). EXCERPTS:
   Beloved Gerry, Rog & Rogie, Daughter your beautiful letter of two

---

*Enclosed was an article from The Washington *Evening Star*, July 15, 1943: In WWII General Douglas MacArthur was a commander of the Rainbow (so named because it was made up troops from 26 states). The reactivated Rainbow Division would now draw its troops from all the states. At its inception ceremony it proudly flew the flags of every state in the Union as it stood at attention to hear the formal order recreating it. General MacArthur, from his Southwest Pacific headquarters, declared that in the Rainbow Division of the World War one felt "an inherent belief that it could not fail in any mission assigned to it. May God bless you and aid you."

weeks ago brought tears of happiness to our eyes. It shall be preserved in the family archives. It is like a mother's letter of long long ago. Written shortly before my birth from which she lied. It has been a comfort to me these many years. It was everything to me when I was a homeless orphan. *(Note by Robert Davis: I was told by my father, Roger, that Grandpa treasured a letter written to him by his mother, who died shortly after his birth. We do not know its whereabouts.)* Your dear letter spoke in the same terms. The mother phrases. Women such as my mother, my wife, my daughter Gerry; they are gifts from the Angels to a suffering & benighted world. Without you mankind would soon, very soon, revert to the wild beast. It was such a happy letter that it cheered our souls & our hearts. May our Dear Lord bless you & keep you, your son & husband; you are the salt of the earth and the goodness thereof ... Last Sunday I could not squeeze a moment to write to you. You may guess from that how busy I was ... ¶ ..Did I tell you we were at the Glen last Sunday. Very hot; garden burnt up — what wasn't eaten by bugs — better next year. Dear mother did all she could & I was so busy I could not help her much. I <u>shall</u> do better next Autumn, Winter & Summer so that when you come next Spring the three of us will have ourselves a time. ¶ *(hot in Baltimore also)* Last week Bill really looked 'doggy' but his crest was up! No son of mine would lower his crest — ever. ¶ *(Grandma just sent Roger a fan)* Trust darling mother to do that for her <u>5</u> boys. I being the most incorrigible <u>and</u> getting no better fast ...

Enclosed was a copy of a letter to the Commanding General of the 42nd Rainbow Division from Lt General J. G. Harbord introducing Sheldon as a capable officer and son of Grandpa's, with whom he had served in Mindanao and Jolo in 1904 & 1905. Grandpa wrote in script at the bottom, "This is from my old friend & C.O. of 42 years ago. Still going to the bat for me & my sons. Great is the old army: <u>LOYALTY</u>."

Sunday, September 5, 1943. Grandpa to Roger (6 pages). This profound letter, with Grandpa's further reference to 'that nether shore' (see also October 6, 1942), transcribed in its entirety.

Beloved Gerry & Rog, How we did enjoy our conversation with you this morning. To know you are happy & well & well cared for comprises our utmost happiness in this life. The shades of evening are falling in our lives and so we look with joy & happiness upon the early mornings of your lives and the dawn of Rogie's life. May the blessings of Heaven and our beloved Savior rest upon you three ever and always. It will because you have the Gift from Him of true love and affection. That effaces all the bitterness of life and its uncertainties: for we know we will meet on that shore where there are no more partings when we may see our beloved ones for eternity and always. And so my beloved daughter, son & grandson we may be happy despite the 'slings & arrows of misfortune' if & when they come upon us, because we shall know that we shall all be together and happy upon that nether shore for ever and for ever. But just the same we will have a lot of joy on this mundane sphere such as family gatherings with cabbage & corn bread, champagne, mint juleps, big thick steaks, some good stories & playing with our grandchildren. All of which savors of things ethereal. St. Peter would join us in a mint julep on the lawn and enjoy it — yes! No God or man could fail to do so: ? the Gods on Olympus & their nectar. The historians had it wrong. It was mint juleps!! ¶ I am enclosing Sheldons letters of August 29. Do not let anything happen to these letters. They are his journal. ¶ It would indeed be wonderful Rog darling son if you did have an opportunity to come on from N.Y. You can get a train about every hour. Go down to the station as early as you are free & get on the first train out of N.Y. to Washington on the Penna. Go on the Pullman & sit down anywhere they will find you a seat — 90% good chance being in uniform will help: tell the Pullman conductor you are going to see Mother & Dad, and that Dad is an old soldier of the Spanish American & World War & many banana wars & that you are stopping by to see him. It will almost always work. ¶ Have heard nothing from Bill & Helen this week but I am sure all is well. Before I completed this sentence Bill called in from the Glen. They arrived there late & were just having supper. It was cool & quiet & quite delightful. We may all be able to gather there on the 18th or 19th if you can get on from N.Y. If only darling Gerry & Rogie could come. But that will come about in due time & we will have a wonderful time there. Rogie can have all the range he needs & that is a lot of range: he being a westerner & husky that way. Nippie & Rogie — what a combination that will be. A boy, a dog and plenty of range. That is near Heaven as a human could be. That dear children of mine awaits us in the not too distant future. ¶ Gerry darling we are so proud & happy in you giving us a fine vigorous grandson. You can scarcely know how deep is our gratification and how we long to know him better & have him know Gran & Pappy & to have & hold him close to our hearts. Rog dear son I am shy of babies — now isn't that strange. No one could love them more deeply than I but I am shy of them. Give Rogie & I a couple of days together and we would be devoted pals & love each other devotedly. But when I first see him again I will be as shy of him as he is of me. You will remember it was so when he was here. Isn't that a queer quirk in grand dad who loves & ? all you four. How I love Rogie is not to be said in words. Just give us two a little time together and you will see devotion almost equal to your own — nothing could equal that of course. Bless your darling loving hearts, all three of you. How I love you I can never tell you. You may get just a glimmering of it from what I do or would I do for you.

Good night beloved Devotedly Dad

SEPTEMBER 12, 1943. GRANDPA TO ROGER (3 PAGES). EXCERPTS:

How nice to hear your wonderful voices — all those this morning. It is a joy to our hearts those Sunday morning talks.. ¶ Gerry & Rog see what you can do in the neighborhood for a room for mother and I. Being very quiet simple people we would be no trouble..we know your hospitality & love for us but it would be crowded and we don't want to do that. We would all be happier if we had a room near you.. It won't be long before we shall be together in Dayton.. we will not be a burden to you..

SUNDAY, OCTOBER 3, 1943. GRANDPA TO ROGER (2 PAGES). EXCERPTS:

.. Mother dear is getting in some horseback riding & looks so well. She can't walk you know — or at least but little and she really requires the exercise. I walk down every morning & that helps a lot. ... ¶ ..enclosing Akin's schedule. A bit stiff isn't it? He is a good student & very steady.. Have to watch him on his exercise. And how about yours, 'Capn'. Gerry, chase him out for it — he needs it. I noted this while he was here. ¶ You will note from Sheldon's letter that they are crowding the 42nd very hard on their training. It means they need the Divisions, or as I take it, that may not be the real reason. The C.O. Genrl may have ants in his pants. He is now a B.G. (one-star, brigadier general) & maybe he is hot after M.S. or Lieuts — could be ... *Letter enclosed from Akin, now a freshman at George Washington University.*

SUNDAY, OCTOBER 10, 1943. GRANDPA TO ROGER (2 PAGES). EXCERPT:

Dear Son & Daughter, Did you note in Sheldon's last letter that he wrote it on the firing range (rifle pits)? If that isn't a challenge to us to write him every week Rog. Soon he will be beyond receiving letters — I know you love him Rog — now is the time to show it before it is too late. I know you will ...

NOVEMBER 1, 1943. GRANDPA TO ROGER (2 PAGES). EXCERPTS:
... Gerry ... we had a real good visit with him even tho it was just one evening. We are so happy that he has gained weight. Keep behind him on the exercise. 15 minutes <u>every</u> day though inadequate will help. If he doesn't get some fresh air & out of door exercise daily he won't keep well ... We spent the day at the Glen & did wish so much for you, & Rog & Rogie. The afternoon was warm & we sat out of doors in the sun!!..
Enclosed is letter from the Marquis Company. Grandpa has suggested Roger's name for "Who's Who."

SUNDAY, NOVEMBER 28, 1943. GRANDPA TO ROGER (4 PAGES). EXCERPTS:
.. No letter from Sheldon this week. He is in the field. Tough going but that is what they are training them for. You read his last letter & hope you have forwarded to Bill. He said the ground was darn hard & believe you me it is. When you get thoroughly inured to it however you can(t) sleep in a bed any more! ¶ .. Mother & Akin at the Glen this morning..I could not go out this week having so much work to do.. ¶ Mother planning to go out to see you *(in)* December.. I cannot get away in December as I had planned. I am as busy as a hen on a hot griddle ...

DECEMBER 19, 1943. GRANDPA TO ROGER (4 PAGES). LETTER TRANSCRIBED IN ITS ENTIRETY.
Dearest Rog, Gerry & Rogie, A right happy and merry Christmas to you my darling little family. ¶ Since we cannot be with you on this day of all days in the year when it is ? that families should be together and since we cannot even talk to you on the telephone, this is the Christmas letter. ¶ We shall be with you in spirit around the Christmas tree and shall join our thoughts and prayers and hearts with yours in the happiness that is yours & no less ours in having a son and heir of so goodly proportions. Son & daughter I know how proud you are of your son & thereby our hearts swell with pride & joy when you look upon him & hold him to your hearts. ¶ How it takes dear mother and me back over the years to the first Christmas tree we ever had with a babe to stare delightfully at

Gerry, Roger and Rogie, Christmastime 1943. At right, Roger's wearing his Dondero trenchcoat, which was a present from Grandpa the previous Christmas.

it: how greatly we enjoyed all the Christmases that have followed in our family life that has been so closely knitted. We know how you dwell in your imaginations upon Rogie's future and how you plan for him & build your hopes upon him. Gerry when Rog went to Princeton Dr. Sidwell, headmaster of Friends School said of him, 'he will be a great comfort to you' and indeed he has. Never has he given us a moments sorrow but has ever & always been a loving & dutiful son. He will be the same husband & father, ever loyal, ever directed and ever thoughtful of your safety and comfort. We are so grateful to Heaven that he has a wife who will be all these things to him & to you & to Rogie. So you see dear daughter how near you, Rog & Rogie are to us and you just as near & perhaps even near(er). Did you not bring us Rogie & haven't you made us all so happy? ¶ And so may our dear Lord guide & keep you safe and may we be together often in the years to come to love & cherish one another. Beloved children of my heart good night and may Peace on Earth & Goodwill to Men once again reign upon Earth.

Ever your devoted Dad

ENCLOSED WAS
A LETTER FROM
AKIN, WHO WAS IN
WASHINGTON WITH
GRANDPA. IN ITS
ENTIRETY:

I sure wish we could all be together again this Christmas like the summer of 1941, but that wouldn't be right because Gerry wasn't with us then. Anyway I wish we could all be together. ¶ My vacation begins Wednesday and lasts until Monday the third of January. It appears that it will be the only vacation I will get until next winter because we don't get a spring vacation and medical school starts a

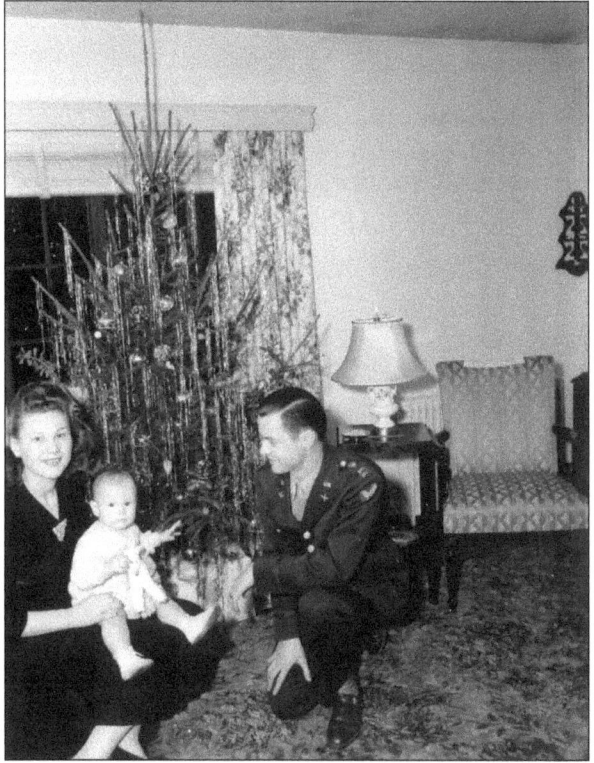

Christmastime 1943.

few days after the last summer session classes. Also there is no time off before either of the two summer sessions. It doesn't sound very pleasing but I guess I can stand it. Maybe I will join the army to get a rest. ¶ I just earned thirty dollars by driving children to and from Mrs. Cook's School. One of my fraternity brothers works there and happened to tell me, about three weeks ago, that Mrs. Cook needed a driver to bring the children to school in the morning and take them home at night. The ones I carry around are about eight years old so I will be able to hold my own against your youngster in a few years. The routes take only about an hour a day so I am paid very well for what I do. I get to school in time every morning so it doesn't interfere at all. ¶ Washington is really dead this Christmas as compared to other Christmases. There are no parties given by those of my age because there is nobody to come to them except girls. As far as I can tell there will be three or four boys who made up the group of forty or fifty boys last winter who will be here next week. It will be a big day when they get together again.

Best wishes, Akin

JANUARY 6, 1944. GRANDPA TO ROGER (1 PAGE). IN ITS ENTIRETY,
Dear Son and Daughter and Grandson Rogie, I don't know whether I remembered to thank you for your thoughtful gift for Christmas. I have thanked you a great many times to myself. You know I have a weakness for hankies and ties, which evidently you remembered. I never open the top drawer of my dresser without thinking of your loving kindness. Your Mother and I think we are very lucky parents to have such sons and daughters. ¶ Rog, I think this will interest you and I want you to put it in your files. Mr. Otto Webber, Head of Personnel in the Santa Monica Douglas Plant; he is a cousin of Mrs. H. Morris Cole, 118 East 6th Street, Los Angeles. This cousin's son is a patient of mine who came into the office yesterday. They are typical Los Angelesians and said when the war was over you might want to get back to Douglas and they would be right on the job to help you. Don't lose this name and address as it might come in handy. ¶ We are making our plans and counting the days until we get on our way for the west. Fondest love from your Mother and me to little Rogie, Geraldine and yourself.   Always devotedly, Dad
Two newspaper articles included. One dated October 23, 193? titled Examination of the Eye Found to Reveal First Sign of Hardening of the Arteries — W.T.D. gives his professional opinion as to why the eye is the window to the entire body. The other dated Oct 21, 1942 titled Battle Toll Traced In Part to Lack of Balance in Schools — W.T.D. gives his opinion as to the failures of our schools to prepare our youth for the battlefield.

JANUARY 1944
Grandma and Grandpa visit Roger, Gerry and Rogie in Dayton. See photos at right and on page 177.

MARCH 12, 1944. GRANDPA TO GERRY (2 PAGES). SHE IS ABOUT TO LEAVE FOR MONTANA FOR A VISIT WITH HER PARENTS. EXCERPT:
.. We are proud of your brother (Bob) as are of you & rightly so. The boys like him are serving our beloved country for your son & his son & my sons & their sons. May our dear Lord shield & protect them for they are the salt of this earth & we love & admire them all ...

January 1944: Grandma and Grandpa Davis with Roger, Gerry and Rogie in Dayton.

SUNDAY, APRIL 2, 1944. GRANDPA TO GERRY (VISITING PARENTS IN MONTANA WITH ROGIE). 4 PAGES.

.. We are so glad you & Rogie are having such a grand time. Give our affectionate regards to your folks and we hope we may have them here some day to get to know them better.. ... ¶ It is very intriguing what you say of Rogie running to the telephone & saying, Dada. Quite a boy. I know the understanding between him and Rog must be very great. Rogie is so responsive and intelligent ... Never shall I forget that day we went for a walk and you and mother let me have him in his buggy. How he made eyes at me and waved his little gloved paw. So friendly and so affectionate. ¶ It is cold & raining & looks as if it might snow tonight. Mother is having a nap in the library and Akin is writing to Sheldon and the house is quiet 'like a mouse'. If Rogie were here we would be so gay ...

Note from Akin end of letter:

Dear Gerry, I know you are enjoying yourself immensely. I cannot fully appreciate your happiness because I have never remained away from home for any length of time but I do know you are having a wonderful time.

Love, Akin

SUNDAY, APRIL 16, 1944. GRANDPA TO ROGER & FAMILY (3 PAGES). EXCERPTS:

.. Don't forget Rog to see General Bevans when the opportunity comes and make an opportunity. My experience over a long life is that most opportunities <u>are made</u> ... Ever always I am watching for the chance to be of help to my sons ... ¶ Rog it is about time for the affair on the coast to be showing up *(Note: he is probably referring to his privileged knowledge of the coming of D-Day — On June 6, 1944, the Allies invaded Western Europe in the largest amphibious attack in history)*; perhaps that is why the delay in the offensive? Might be. General Hines prophecy of the war being over in Europe I suspect was based on that; might be. But it didn't happen. After you fellows read this destroy it. Quickly & completely. ¶ Akin may be in the draft; the confusion of the Selective Service is most distressing. Dirty politics. You may early guess son where it emanates & may God help us. ¶ How wonderful it is to feel we will see you in the last week of May. If you can let me know ahead — well ahead it is possible that Bill & Sheldon may get home for that week ...

Enclosed is letter from Akin. Excerpt: .. Unless there is a big change in the

January 1944: Grandpa walked Rogie in his buggy. "How he made eyes at me and waved his little gloved paw. So friendly and so affectionate."

*Last week of May, 1944. All four boys, with Helen, Gerry and Rogie, visit at
Lowell Street. Photo taken at Grandpa's request. (CLOCKWISE FROM LEFT:
Sheldon, Bill, Roger, Akin.)*

draft law or the opening of med. school, this little note is being written by
a prospective private in the army. Akin

LAST WEEK OF MAY, 1944
*All four boys, and Helen, Gerry and Rogie come home to Lowell Street. Bill,
Roger, Sheldon and Akin have their picture taken together at Buckingham
Studio, Washington, D.C.*

Roger took these last pictures of his mom and dad in the back yard of their Lowell Street home during his visit in the last week of May, 1944.

Last week of May, 1944. Rogie, Gerry, and the grandparents in the back yard at Lowell Street. These pictures are arranged on these two pages just as they were in Roger and Gerry's photo album. Renée wrote to Roger on July 31, 1944: "The pictures taken in the garden were lovely — one is so sweet of Dad and Rogie — and Dad and I don't look too bad. They were of course Dad's last. There is so much to talk about that I cannot put into words."

SUNDAY, JUNE 4, 1944. GRANDPA TO GERRY, ROG & ROGIE. IN ITS EN-TIRETY.

Dearest Gerry, Rog & Rogie, How we miss you & particularly Rogie. The lawn seems empty; the house much too quiet. Mother and I speak of nothing else but of how much we miss him & you both. With all the ? of that week we only remember how dear to our hearts was your visit. We hear the gargantuan laughs on the lawn, the sweet bird-like voice of Rogie, his digging in the mud & throwing of stones. A real He lad he is; patience with him my darlings; he is a wonderful boy — a boy — a he boy. Don't curb him <u>too</u> much. A he, red blooded little <u>man</u> is he. Give him all the room you can. His heart is right. ¶ We just enjoyed a talk with you <u>dear</u> ones; how grateful we are for this EACH WEEK to hear your voices and to know all is well with you. 'Tis a satisfaction so deep it may not be expressed in words. May our dear Lord bless & keep you beloved of my heart.

Ever devotedly Dad

Just had a wire from Sheldon; he has his promotion — 1st Lieutenant. A note would be in order or perhaps a wire.

JUNE 8, 1944. GRANDPA'S APPRECIATION LETTER TO COL. SIMS.
Grandpa writes to express appreciation for a letter from Col. Sims commending Roger on his promotion to the rank of Major. In the words of Col. Sims, "This promotion was granted only due to this (these) exceptional abilities and qualifications: a son, officer and a gentleman." After Grandpa's death, Col. Sims very thoughtfully gave Roger Grandpa's letter, in its original envelope, along with his own personal note observing how proud Grandpa had been of his son (see following page).

LAST LETTER. JUNE 10, 1944. GRANDPA TO ROGER, GERRY, AND ROGIE
On Saturday, June 10, 1944 Grandpa wrote his last letter to Roger, Gerry and Rogie. Akin wrote a note at the end of this letter. Transcribed below in its entirety:
3601 Lowell St. N.W. Washington 16 D. C.
Saturday, June 10, '44
Dear Rog & Gerry & Rogie,

Aren't we proud of our Rog. This letter is a rare treasure. It touches our hearts. I have written Col. Sims but had no words to express my appreciation. It was wonderful of him. 'This promotion was granted only due

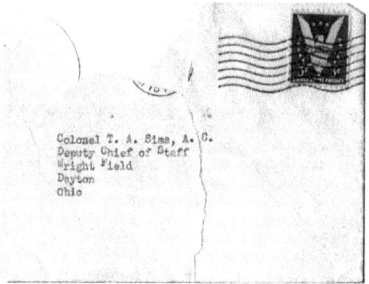

WM. THORNWALL DAVIS, M. D
ERNEST SHEPPARD, M. D.
927 SEVENTEENTH STREET N. W.
WASHINGTON 6, D. C.

June 8, 1944

Colonel T. A. Sims, A.C.
Deputy Chief of Staff
Wright Field
Dayton, Ohio

My dear Colonel Sims:

    I do want to express Mrs. Davis' and my deepest
appreciation for your letter of June 6, 1944. We really
have not words to say how deep our appreciation is.

    What you said about our son could only be under-
stood from one officer of the old Army to another; it
has a meaning to us that it would not have to others.
It is very thoughtful of you to take of your time from
your very busy life to write us. We often speak of you
and Roger often writes of you; he is devoted to you and
he always speaks of you in terms of the highest affection
and esteem.

    I hope you will not forget that the latchstring
is on the outside for you if and when you come to
Washington. The boys are all in the service now and
we have plenty of room and will not curtail your activities in any way.

    Again with appreciation for your kindness, and
with warm personal regards, believe me,

Most sincerely yours,

WTD:rk

Col. Sims gave Roger Grandpa's letter, along with a personal note.

to this (these) exceptional abilities and qualifications: a son, officer and a
gentleman'. That is a message from an officer of the old army to another
of the same type. Nothing could have cheered & warmed my heart as this
did. It is the highest military compliment that could possibly be given you
Major Davis beloved son of mine. Preserve it carefully in your archives for
your son & his son & beyond that. I am enclosing a copy for you. Put the
original carefully away. I think of sending copies to Gen York, Mrs. Arnold, Mr. Spillsbury, Uncle Bat do you agree? Would Col. Sims be pleased?
Any others you would desire? *(See page 184 for the photo of Roger as Major.)*

    You will wish to thank Col. Sims saying I sent you <u>a copy</u> of his letter?
Perhaps you might say, if agreeable to you, Dad would like to send a letter

to Gen York my friend and a fellow Kentuckian, Gen Arnold one of my old friends in the army with whom I served, & the former Surgeon General Patterson *(Bob Patterson, "Battle-Axe Bob")* with whom I served in the Moro Campaigns. You need not mention your brothers or Mr. Spillsbury since these are of the family. I shall not send out my other letters until I hear from you. One must proceed carefully as you with your great intelligence will appreciate.

So nice to hear your voice on Friday — we appreciate your calling dear son knowing how pressed for time you were. Hope I did not keep you too long; I fear I did. Darling mother is so deeply happy at your great compliment. It has been a happy WEEK: Sheldon & you promoted, such a nice & happy letter from Bill, and Akin has just returned from W. R. H. (Walter Reed Hosp) Army Medical Center after been examined by Col (Dr. King) professor of Cardiology & Johns Hopkins & one of the leading cardiologists in the country who says Akin's heart murmur is purely functional and may be completely ignored. So it has been a week of deep happiness to your dear mother and to me. Our sons taking their place in the world, serving their country honorably & well. Duty could be so satisfactory; nothing could give us deeper happiness.

Our fondest love to your dear wife and our darling grandson. We miss you all so much. More power to you son; at your age you have made a good sound start in your life. May it ever be happier and more deeply satisfactory to you.

Ever devotedly, Dad

Akin wrote this on the last page:

Dear Rog, It was swell talking to you for a few seconds the other day although I didn't have time to say anymore than congratulations. I would like to say again how proud we are of you. Not many people I know can boast a Major as a brother. ¶ I have some very good news to tell you about me now. This afternoon I had an appointment with Col. King at Walter Reed. He is an excellent heart specialist and after examining me said there was nothing at all wrong with me except a completely insignificant noise caused by contact of my heart with part of a lung. Needless to say it was a great load off my mind to learn that I will be able to get into the army.

Akin

Roger promoted to Major. Roger wrote at bottom left of this photo, "To the most wonderful wife in the world. With all my love, Rog."

THREE DAYS AFTER THE LAST LETTER: TUESDAY, JUNE 13, 1944.
As part of his daily exercise Grandpa always walked home after work (3.5 miles to their home on Lowell St.). Inclement weather on this day did not deter his strong will and his good habit. He walked, refusing offers for rides from passersby. With a history of heart problems, he had a heart attack that evening. As a doctor he had observed and understood the crippling effects of serious heart condition. He had expressed to certain members of his family before this that he did not want to be a "burden" to his family as a "heart cripple."

THREE DAYS LATER, FRIDAY, JUNE 16, 1944.
Grandpa, William Thornwall Davis, had his second heart attack and died at his home on Lowell Street in the presence of Renée and Akin. He was 67 years old (Renée age 57, Bill 30, Roger 27, Sheldon 22, and Akin 19). Grandpa's clothes had been meticulously laid out by his bed ready for him to be off again to his work and duties. He lived and died by principle, loyalty, love and duty. Per his obituary, "He went as he would probably have wished, suddenly, in the midst and at the peak of his brilliant, varied and fruitful career."

Grandpa had misgivings about certain ministers in the "church" so Grandma asked Grandpa's good friend, Rev. Frederick Von der Sump to conduct the funeral service. Mr. Von (as the family knew him) was the owner/operator of their summer vacation spot at Camp Vonhurst. Mr. Von came by train from New Hampshire but had so little money he had to borrow to travel. He had no money to return so Renée paid his travel expenses to and from New Hampshire. The funeral service was held at their Lowell Street home. Rev. Von der Sump spoke about Grandpa's beliefs and his ideals — his hatred of hypocrisy and second rate things — his ever striving for his ideals — his utter devotion to his family. He delivered two quotations that expressed Grandpa's beliefs: 1) Taken from the Scriptures — "We brought nothing into this world, and it is certain we can carry nothing out. The Lord gave, and the Lord hath taken away; blessed be the name of the Lord." 2) A Persian Proverb — "A Man Who Hath Children Never Dies."

Dr. Thornwall Davis, Noted Eye Specialist, Dies of Heart Disease

Dr. William Thornwall Davis, 67, noted eye specialist, professor and senior surgeon of the Episcopal Eye, Ear and Throat Hospital, died last night shortly after he was stricken with a heart attack at his home, 3601 Lowell street N.W.

Dr. Davis was a consulting ophthalmologist at Garfield, Columbia, Gallinger, Casualty and George Washington University Hospitals. Since 1920 he has served as professor of ophthalmology at George Washington University. During the World War, with the rank of major, he had held a similar post at the Army Medical School. He was a member of the Advisory Board to selective service in 1941.

Nephew of Senator Blackburn.

Dr. Davis, nephew of the late Senator Blackburn, Democrat, of Kentucky and a native of Little Rock, Ark., received his M. D. degree at George Washington University in 1901. He attended the Army Medical School, the University of Vienna and the Royal Ophthalmic Hospital in London. He served his internship at Garfield Hospital. His private office was located at 927 Farragut square.

From 1902 to 1913, Dr. Davis served in the Army Medical Corps, entering the service with the rank of first lieutenant, later being promoted to captain.

Dr. Davis was a Fellow of the American College of Surgeons and member of the American Medical Association, Southern Medical Association, American Academy of Ophthalmolgy and Otolaryngology, the Pan-American Medical Association and the Academy of Medicine, Washington.

Member of Military Orders.

He also served as a member of the Board of Directors of the Washington Loan & Trust Co., and belonged to the Military Order of the Caraboa, Spanish-American War Veterans, American Legion, Rotary Club and the Masons. He was a member of the Army and Navy, Metropolitan and Chevy Chase Clubs.

Mr. Davis is survived by his widow, Mrs. Renee Tolson Davis, and four sons, Dr. William J. G. Davis, Cleveland, Ohio; Maj. Roger Has Brouck Davis, Army Air Forces, now stationed at Wright Field, Dayton, Ohio; First Lt. Rene S. Davis, U. S. A., now at Camp Gruber, Okla., and Akin Thornwall Davis, a premedical student at George Washington University.

Arrangements for the funeral have not yet been completed.

DR. WILLIAM THORNWALL DAVIS.
—Harris & Ewing Photo.

Renée continued to live at 3601 Lowell St. in Washington with Akin. Vivian, who had nannied the four boys and worked in the household for 30 years, continued to work for Grandma. Della also remained as cook. Roger and Gerry and family visited often. (Note: the last Davis visit to Camp Vonhurst was by Renée and Akin in 1945). Renée died December 27, 1968 (81 years old).

Bill joined the Army Medical Corps in 1945 after his internship at Johns Hopkins. After serving at Walter Reed and West Point he was discharged as a Captain in 1947. He opened his ophthalmology practice in Washington at the Farragut Square office. He and Helen lived and maintained his practice in Washington until his death from heart attack in 1968 at the age of 54. Joel Boone wrote after his death, "He was such a buoyant, alive, cheerful, animated person exhibiting zestfulness of life. There was always the ready smile on his handsome countenance. He was a perfect gentleman with courtly manners. He was a man of highest honor. He was a physician who loved his profession and brought honor to it as well as distinction." After his death Dad gave me a number of letters written to his wife, Helen, which spoke of the deep honor and respect people had for Bill. Dad wrote, "I know you will treasure these letters as do I."

Sheldon served in Europe with the 42nd Rainbow Division. He married Alyse Maxine Denise during his Army service. Sheldon fought in the Battle of the Bulge (December 16, 1944 – January 25, 1945, the last major German offensive of World War II) and in the closing days of WW11 engaged in the liberation of a major subcamp of Dachau concentration camp (April 1945). During his stay at Dachau Sheldon found an emaciated German Shepherd, one of the Nazi camp guard dogs left behind by the retreating German Army. He slowly and carefully nursed this dog back to health, eventually gaining its trust and friendship. He named him King and shipped him home to Grandma to become the family pet. Rogie and Bob remember playing with King as young children in Grandma's back yard. Sheldon's wife, Maxine, died (1946) in Germany before Sheldon returned to the United States. After the war he worked for Anaconda Copper Mining Company in Butte, Montana. Sheldon remarried to Ann Maxine McLaughlin, moved to Florida and had three sons: William Oliver Davis, Joseph Sheldon Davis, and James Perry Davis. Sheldon led a difficult life. He died of heart problems August 27, 1980, at the age of 59.

Roger and Gerry had three children: Roger HB. Davis, Jr., myself (Robert Graham Davis), and Sheryl Renée Davis. Roger had been promoted by his commanding officer to Major due to his exceptional abilities and qualifications as a "son, officer and gentleman." His personal and professional life always reflected the same — he was a grateful and loyal son, the perfect father, a loving and loyal husband, a gentleman — love and success followed him throughout his life. Roger died in 2004 at the age of 87, ten years after receiving triple bypass heart surgery. Roger and Gerry were married 62 years. Mom died peacefully August 14, 2011, at the age of 93 in the presence of family. I will write a separate biography on my Dad and Mom.

King, a German shepherd Sheldon rescued from a Nazi prison camp and shipped home to become the family pet.

Akin graduated from St. Albans Preparatory School in 1943. He attended George Washington University, was drafted into the Army as an infantryman in 1945 and separated from the service in 1946. After the service he attended University of Delaware doing undergraduate study in chemical engineering. His college years were again interrupted when he was called back into the service (1950–1951), serving in Japan during the Korean War. He married Cari (Carterette Cheetam) in 1951. Akin graduated from University of Delaware in 1953 and worked for Dupont Co. in Aiken, South Carolina from 1953 to 1956. He returned to Washington, worked for the U.S. Patent Office, attending George Washington night law school for four years to obtain his law degree. He worked as a patent attorney in Washington until his retirement in 1989. Akin and Cari had three boys: Christopher Akin Davis, Garrett Vail Davis, and Graham Lake Davis. Presently he continues to enjoy his retirement, living in the same house in which they raised their

three boys, at 3941 Legation Street, NW, Washington, D.C.

Eleven months after Grandpa's passing, May 28, 1945, Roger's second son, Robert G. Davis, was born. I never had the privilege of knowing my Grandfather because I was born a year after his passing, but when we were young, I, Rogie and Sheryl were told many stories by Dad and Uncle Bill about his exploits, accomplishments and extraordinary character. It has been one of the great honors of my life to write this book. Through the letters between Grandpa and my dad I feel I have succeeded in bringing him (as well as my dad) back to life and in getting to know him better than I ever could have imagined. I do hope I have been able to do so for you also. His inspiration has been a major contributor to the development of my courage and will to persevere and pursue duty. He stated many times, "A Man Who Hath Children Never Dies"; and indeed he still and will always live, because born from his son, and from Grandpa's incredible will to overcome great adversity and live a complete and fulfilling life in service to his family, country, and humanity, I, Robert G. Davis, have always carried him as a part of me, as I believe have his other grandchildren. I now hope our children and their children will do the same. I draw on his strength and his indomitable will and discipline to persevere, succeed and pursue duty. Inside he is my cheerleader, my spiritual banner, my battle cry to arms for the high standard, nobility and unrelenting determination of our family. He and Christopher Columbus Graham are the two most principled and accomplished people known to me in our family history. Grandpa wrote in his letters to Roger, "May our dear Lord save you for the future good of family and country." He also wrote, "It is well for you to know you have ancestry of education and culture. The aristocracy of America, that is what bears you up in time of stress. See to it that you do not dissipate it in your progeny." Well, his sons WERE saved for the good of their families and their country and we, his progeny, WILL NOT dissipate the love, wisdom and education of those who came before us and made us who we are. We can be proud of where we came from, we can be proud of who and what we are, and yes, Grandfather, we WILL pass it on to our progeny. I am moved to say, as my final thought in this writing, that I pray that one day, Grandpa, Mom, Dad, and all those whom I love will meet on that "nether shore of no more partings."

FOLLOWING are transcripts and excerpts of letters from Renée to Roger, July 31, 1944 through May 5, 1951.

JULY 31, 1944. GRANDMA TO ROGER (AT 537 DAYTON PARKWAY, DAYTON, OHIO). EXCERPTS:
.. I'm counting the days until your visit ... Dr. Shepherd has taken over the office. Will pay me rent for the building and the instruments. This as of July 1st. This rent with the rent of McGill Terrace will carry everything and no money will have to be borrowed as the estate will be settled before the usual time. ... The pictures taken in the garden *(end of May)* were lovely — one is so sweet of Dad and Rogie — and Dad and I don't look <u>too</u> bad. I an so glad to have them. They are of course Dad's last ...

AUGUST 21, 1944. GRANDMA TO ROGER. THIS LETTER IN ROGER'S KEEP-SAKE FILE. IN IT'S ENTIRETY.
Dearest Rog, A week has gone by since you left. We have all missed you. You are truly part of me dear Rog. ¶ Rogie is a darling and <u>so cute</u> and sweet. I don't think your Gerry has been <u>too</u> bored but of course she has missed you and her own home. However, the rest has benefited her, I think. She <u>eats</u> and rests. A long rest in the afternoon. It was kind and generous of you to do without your dear ones. It has kept me from being too lonely. ¶ Your bank account must be getting low. A trip home is always on us as dear Dad would say. We always want it that way and it will be that way, dear son, as long as there is enough and there always will be enough for that always. A great deal of love.

Affectionately, Mommie

SEPTEMBER 7, 1944. GRANDMA TO ROGER. EXCERPTS:
... Leonard is on his vacation. Will be back the 15th. Vivian is then going home. When she returns I'll let Leonard go. I hate to tell him. I know he can get a place with more money but I think he is devoted to the family and has stayed on that account ... Think over what is best to do with the Packard, Rog. I don't imagine there would be much sale for so large and heavy a car but perhaps in Washington some of these newcomers here would want a swanky car. I don't imagine there will be many large cars manufactured after the war — every one will want a light one. 'I dun no'. Perhaps after the European finish we will have more gas. ¶ Things are going very well at

the office. The only trouble is that there are too many patients. ... Shep is carrying on well — he must slow up tho. He can't take it as our Daddy did for so many years. In August his net income was $2,900. He is wise enough to know it won't keep up that way for much longer and so is not going haywire. I'm glad of this. ¶ Della got religion over Sunday and Monday and is running in circles. It seems the Father Grace (colored), who has her under his thumb had a large outdoor meeting and baptized the recruits with a garden hose. Fire department wouldn't lend the hose this year. It cost them a dollar a wetting besides spoiling their shoes. Such a racket. Love to all,

Affectionately Mother

October 22, 1944. Grandma to Roger. In its entirety:

Dearest children, A long letter arrived on Thursday from Sheldon. In many respects a very nice letter — very manly and to me very pitiful. He was married to Maxine *(the girl who drove his car to Benning)* on July 3rd. I want you to write him at once and wish him happiness — tell him some small bit of news etc. Just a brotherly letter. Please do not mention his method of marriage or mention me at all. Any words of blame would cause a rift in the family. He is leaving shortly — he needs us all and we must stand behind him. I wrote him at once. I sent him my blessing and the fervent wish that they would be very happy. There must be no ill thoughts and no words said that hurt him or make him feel anything but happiness before he leaves. Between his lines there is to me a great sadness. He speaks of his great happiness and his sorrow and shame that he didn't let me know. He feels after four months that he has made no mistake. For my sake write him at once — both of you. ¶ My love, dear ones — God! How I ache. This I shall never mention it again — It will be said only to my children. No one else must know.

Affectionately Mother

July 27, 1945. Grandma to Roger. Excerpt:
She is at Vonhurst. Asks For Gerry, Rogie and Bobby to take a train to Washington to visit and give Rogie space to run safely in a yard. Vivian will take care of him. She wants to see the newborn, Bobby. Excerpt:

.. I had a wire or cable last week from Sheldon. I quote 'Disregard letters — effect a transfer to Stark immediately. Urgent.' This worries me as I'm afraid he has gotten in Dutch with his regimental enemies — but I'm trying to believe that he has heard that the 42nd is to remain indefinitely in the Austrian Tyrol and he is not happy in the thought of being there and wants to be on his way. *(General Stark is a friend of the family.)*

OCTOBER 13, 1945. GRANDMA TO ROGER. EXCERPTS:

Vivian was delighted with Gerry's letter but didn't feel she should take the enclosure but I assured her she should as she needs it to help on a dentist's bill.. ¶ This letter will give you a shock and jolt and will cause you grief and anger but I feel you should know what has happened ... I called Dr. Sheppard concerning his lease which was up in July and we made an appointment.. When he came he opened up on me; said he had no intention of paying such a rent — that the lease was cold-blooded, calculating, unfair, ungrateful and he was tired of supporting 3601 Lowell Street and didn't intend to do it. He then opened up on Dad, was most unkind, cruel and disrespectful. He said he didn't owe Dad <u>anything</u>, he didn't owe the office anything and he didn't owe me anything and that he was leaving 927 *(Farragut Square office)*, cutting all ties with it. I asked him if he was repudiating all the understanding and the fact that Bill was to go in with him *(Bill will soon be out of the army)*. He just shrugged his shoulders and when I demanded an answer he said, 'Oh, if Bill still wishes to he can come work for me.' He said Dad's office meant nothing to him that he didn't need the goodwill — he didn't need to have people know that he had associated with Dad ... *(Grandma goes on about this — Bill was there and witnessed all of this)* ... He has completely lost his reason, his heart and his soul. I think you will be proud to know that I did not lose my temper. I spoke quietly and to the point. The money he made in the year has gone to his head.. enormous income ... I keep in mind and heart his years of hard work and loyalty to Dad and interest in Bill and Akin. ... How can money so change a person? I think he feels that here is a gold mine — of my working — I have actualized all this — I am great, I am influential. ... I feel perhaps it is all for the best. Much better to have known what he is before Bill went in with him. The only thing that keeps hurting is to have Dad's life work, his inheritance to his sons, and his living monument torn down and thrown away just on account of this great souled man. It seems impossible doesn't it? It means that Bill will have to begin at the beginning. This I feel will be of benefit to him. He has never had to stand on his two feet and he has never had any real responsibility. For him to start new, by himself, will be an education for him and will benefit him. I hope Dad is not looking down and seeing what has taken place. We are going to ride this storm out and so help me God Dad's life work is not going to tumble to earth. We will keep Dad's office and keep some of the girls ... during the time Bill is in the Army. The office will be there with someone on duty — the lights will burn and the flag will fly — it has been out every National Holiday and it has been out to greet the returning servicemen. I'll have to stop for a minute — the tears are falling down like rain ... I wish you could be here so that I could talk everything over with you, Rogie pie. Excuse all the doleful tone.

Love to you all. Mother

MARCH 4, 1946. GRANDMA TO ROGER. EXCERPTS:
... last week we went to the Wednesday evening concert. Vivian has a season ticket and she and Maxine sit together ... *(Grandma is still renting the McGill Terrace house — also is renting the Glen.)*

JUNE 21, 1946. GRANDMA TO ROGER (AT 917 EAST 77TH STREET, KANSAS CITY, MISSOURI).
Copy and explanation of her will.

DECEMBER 1, 1949. GRANDMA TO ROGER (AT 603 FLORIDA AVENUE, OAK RIDGE, TENNESSEE).
Sheldon and Ann have a son. Asks Roger to write to him: You are the only one of the two brothers to understand how he feels. *Grandma very busy socially. Parties and occasions with Generals and friends (including Joel Boone), concerts, luncheons. Lowell St. for sale — if sold no place to go — will have to put King in a kennel. McGill Terrace and Glen still rented.*

MAY 13, 1951. GRANDMA TO ROGER. GRANDMA (AGE 64) LIVING AT 2852 McGILL TERRACE. IN ITS ENTIRETY:
Dear Roger and Gerry, All is well here. Bobby is being a good boy. We have no trouble whatsoever. ⁊ Helen, Bill and 'Lumpy', Helen's nephew, were here for Brunch at 11:30. They always sleep Sunday mornings. A good brunch 'brunch'. Orange juice, fried chicken, hot cakes, coffee. We ate and ate. Bobby had to unfasten the snap on his pants. The syrup just about ran out of his ears. Old King came in for a share of the skin and soft bones, such as the ribs. ⁊ Wonderful day. Just right, the other branch of the Davis

family has now gone to the ball game. Red Sox and some other team. ❡ I think I shall drive up or over to Hagerstown *(Note: Roger, Gerry and family moving from Oak Ridge, Tennessee, to Hagerstown, Maryland — they will now be 73 miles from Washington, D.C.)* on Wednesday if it is a fine day and look the town over. The woods are pretty now and then too I want to get some mileage on the car. I have only been 500 miles — as you see I don't drive much. ❡ Aunt Eleana was here for two days this week. We went to Arlington — Uncle Bob's and Dad's remains are quite close. I think they would like it that way. Young Bob hasn't been called as yet. He is a paratrooper in the Infantry Airborne Division & is a first lieutenant. I hope he will not be called. She would be so alone. ❡ You were very thoughtful to mention the Westinghouse articles. I wish I could afford an ice box, a stove, etc but the two moves in one year and the repairs and re-doing here has put me in the red. ... the bank will hold my checks until the trust fund interest comes in. I'm not worrying about it. ❡ I do think it wise to get a new ice box if you can get the 30% off. Have looked them over and feel the one with an X is best for us. Any one buying or renting the house would have more than one in family. The one here is very good but is eleven years old and had three lots of tenants and is a little beat up. I can probably sell it and that will help on the payment. Also would like an electric oven if you can get a percentage on that. Let me know what they will cost and I'll send you a check right away. ❡ Vivian home today, the first since May 15. The head maid at the Club was taken ill and the manager simply told Vivian she would have to take over. Which she did. I was a little burned up about it but Vivian goes off her head you know and said she had to take her as she owed it to the Club and she couldn't leave the Club in the lurch. You know how she is when she gets off on the wrong foot. There is no doubt about it she saved the day. The maid returns tonight and Vivian is more dead than alive. Then on the job at 8:30 AM. and on her feet until 10 at night. Bobby and King and she are now going for a walk in the Park. We are only one block from Rock Creek Park. This evening they are going to the Shoreham to see the fountain with the colored lights playing on it. There will be music too. Bobby seems very pleased. ❡ Mr. Coe, our next door neighbor is doing quite a lot of repairs — not too noisy tho as all is inside work except the garage roof and the tearing off of the porch. His butler or good man Friday is very pleasant and says he is sorry etc and hopes I will forgive him — Don't know what nationality he is. ❡ Did I tell you Mrs. Brett was here for two or three days? She sent her love to 'Rogie Pie'. ¶ Joel is back but Helen is in Menlo Park. All three of Suzie's children have the measles and Suzie came down with them so Helen really landed in a hard job. However the little girls are wonderful and the boy, age 16 months is a strong, happy boy. ¶ By now I hope your Daddy has recovered Gerry. Real operations are no fun. I never want to go to another hospital. ¶ A letter from Akin sounds cheerful. The countryside is beautiful with both flowers and trees. Lots of our poor boys have come in from Korea. Morale wonderful. I just don't listen to the commentators anymore or the debates on this and that except the MacArthur and Marshall news. All very confusing. Truman talk on Defense was worse than nothing. Much as I hate to side with him I'm not for stirring up Russia — If we did our troops in Europe would be goners overnight. The anti British feeling is quite apparent. Of course they are trying to save their necks and economy. Their rubber and other materials going to red China is going to cause more friction here. Especially the lame answer that it is <u>only</u> going to the civilians. We are dumb but not <u>that</u> dumb. Everyone here thinks that it was wise in Churchill not to come at this time. He would have been asked some pretty blunt questions. But who am I to mumble on.

Lots of love to you all. Affectionately Mother

That was Grandma's last letter to Mom and Dad.

ABOUT THE AUTHOR

Robert Graham Davis is the second grandchild of William Thornwall Davis, having been born one year after his passing. Bob regards it as among the great honors of his life to write this book about his grandfather, one of the most extraordinary people in his ancestry. Through the letters between W. T. Davis and his son Roger (Bob's dad), he feels he has gotten to know his grandfather better than he could ever have imagined.

Bob lives in Charlottesville, Virginia, with his wife, Barbara. They have four children and eight grandchildren. He and his brother, Roger HasBrouck Davis, Jr. — the only grandchild that their grandfather ever knew — worked together in the real estate business for forty years.